## Praise for Tavis Smiley's
# DEATH OF A KING

"Smiley's King is at once more flawed and more human than we have come to see him. But for that reason he is even more courageous, and more admirable."
—Clay Risen, *New York Times Book Review*

"Tavis Smiley brings the civil rights leader's humanity, imperfections, passions, and political struggles into focus."
—Carolyn Kellogg, *Los Angeles Times*

"A reverential look at Martin Luther King Jr.'s last agonizing year that does not disguise the flaws of a saint.... A poignant account of King's final struggle.... An eloquent, emotional journey from darkness to light."
—*Kirkus Reviews*

"Tavis Smiley has captured not only the spirit of the movement, but the spirit of Martin Luther King Jr. in his last days. We didn't realize it, but he knew he was on his way to Jerusalem, and as much as we tried to deter him, he fought back."
—Andrew Young, former U.S. ambassador to the United Nations and former mayor of Atlanta

"*Death of a King* is a fitting climax to a noble saga. It is here adequately told and placed before history."
—Reverend Gardner C. Taylor

"A microscopically focused biography, which trades in both weighty events and the everyday joys of family life."

—*Time*

"Tavis Smiley has brought forward in his book *Death of a King* an accounting of the last year Dr. King was physically with us—an accounting very much needed. Tavis rightfully emphasizes the error it is to continually emphasize his martyrdom mostly with no mention of the great work he did. Tavis's book helps people focus on his work and the spirit with which he worked."

—Dorothy F. Cotton, education director for SCLC, the organization led by Dr. King

"Gripping.... The worth of *Death of a King* lies in its story, succinctly and achingly told." —Scott Porch, *Daily Beast*

"Smiley has a great ability to get deep into the mystery of a person and uncover what lies beneath. With *Death of a King,* Smiley looks beyond the myth of King to craft a portrayal both honest and respectful. A unique addition to the King pantheon." —Hope Wabuke, *The Root*

"Meticulously researched.... A powerful tribute."

—Wendy Werris, *Publishers Weekly*

"Heartfelt and accessible."

—Sarah Murdoch, *Toronto Star*

"An important work that, if taken seriously, can transform the current narrative into an authentic one if King is to truly be the nation's moral conscience."
—Byron Williams, *Huffington Post*

"Tavis Smiley illuminates the passion and struggle of Martin Luther King Jr.'s last 365 days." *—AARP*

"*Death of a King* paints a portrait of a leader and visionary in a revealing and dramatic chronicle of the twelve months leading up to King's assassination."
—Nicole M. Robertson, *Oakland Press*

"This book by PBS host Smiley shows a very different world for King....He is, in this book, not a plaster saint but a multi-dimensional man....The writing technique succeeds in making the story more immediate, King more approachable."
—Alan Rosenberg, *Providence Journal*

"Masterfully crafted....Insightful and uplifting....A powerful testament to the life of a great man."
—Charles Shea LeMone, *Roanoke Times*

## ALSO BY TAVIS SMILEY

*My Journey with Maya*

*The Rich and the Rest of Us*

*Fail Up*

*Accountable*

*The Covenant with Black America*

*The Covenant in Action*

*What I Know for Sure*

*Never Mind Success—Go for Greatness!*

*Keeping the Faith*

*Doing What's Right*

*Hard Left*

*How to Make Black America Better*

*On Air*

*Just a Thought*

# DEATH
## OF A
# KING

*The Real Story of
Dr. Martin Luther King Jr.'s
Final Year*

## TAVIS SMILEY

### WITH DAVID RITZ

Back Bay Books
Little, Brown and Company
New York   Boston   London

Back Bay Books / Little, Brown and Company
Hachette Book Group
1290 Avenue of the Americas, New York, NY 10104
littlebrown.com

Originally published in hardcover by Little, Brown and Company, September 2014
First Back Bay paperback edition, January 2016

Back Bay Books is an imprint of Little, Brown and Company. The Back Bay Books name and logo are trademarks of Hachette Book Group, Inc.

The publisher is not responsible for websites (or their content) that are not owned by the publisher.

The Hachette Speakers Bureau provides a wide range of authors for speaking events. To find out more, go to hachettespeakersbureau.com or call (866) 376-6591.

"Tribute to a King" lyrics courtesy of William Bell / Booker T. Jones

Library of Congress Cataloging-in-Publication Data

Smiley, Tavis
    Death of a King : the real story of Dr. Martin Luther King Jr.'s final year / Tavis Smiley with David Ritz. — First edition.
        pages cm
    Includes bibliographical references and index.
    ISBN 978-0-316-33276-7 (hardcover) / 978-0-316-41065-6 (large print) / 978-0-316-33277-4 (paperback)
    1. King, Martin Luther, Jr., 1929–1968.   2. African American civil rights workers—Biography.   3. African Americans—Civil rights—History—20th century.   I. Ritz, David.   II. Title.
    E185.97.K5S56 2014
    323.092—dc23                                                        2014018814

10  9  8  7  6  5  4  3  2  1

RRD-C

Printed in the United States of America

*For Martin Luther King Jr.... America's greatest*
*democratic public intellectual*

*April is the cruelest month.*

— T. S. ELIOT, *THE WASTE LAND*

# CONTENTS

## PART II
## THE FINAL SEASON: THE LAST
## THREE MONTHS

# DEATH

OF A

# KING

# INTRODUCTION

I hold this project precious for reasons that are both intensely personal and politically urgent.

As a young boy growing up in a trailer park in rural Indiana, my initial encounter with the speeches of Martin Luther King Jr. altered the very course of my life. During the most difficult period of my childhood, a time when I had fallen into deep despair, his spirit entered my soul and excited my imagination. I recognized the rhythms of his rhetorical passion as more than hypnotic: I knew they were righteous. As a result of their disturbing truths, I became a lifelong student of his work as a minister, advocate, and writer. His call to radical democracy through redemptive love resonated with me on a profound level.

I was barely a teenager when I began entering statewide oratorical interpretation competitions by declaiming King's most famous speeches. The thrill of channeling his voice — not to mention my frequent victories — had me believing that my connection to the man was preternatural. It was certainly life affirming. Through the voice of the prophetic minister I eventually found my own voice.

My study of King's pivotal role in the history of this country has never stopped. Over the years, I have spoken with his most important critics, chroniclers, and defenders. I was privileged to enjoy a rewarding friendship with Coretta Scott King, whom I interviewed many times. Her last national television interview was an appearance on my public television program filmed in Atlanta's Ebenezer Baptist Church in 2005, on what would have been her husband's seventy-sixth birthday. At her behest, I served on the advisory board at the Martin Luther King, Jr. Center for Nonviolent Social Change in Atlanta.

Yet for all the years that I have read, discussed, and analyzed King's work, this is the first time I have sought to capture my feelings about him in a book. That's because now, after decades of study, I have come to firmly believe that, in a critical way, he is misunderstood. I further believe that misunderstanding is robbing us of the essence of his character and crusade.

Ironically, his martyrdom has undermined his message. As a public figure who fearlessly challenged the status quo, he has been sanitized and oversimplified. The values for which he lived and died—justice for all, service to others, and a love that liberates, no matter the cost—are largely forgotten. He is no longer a threat, but merely an idealistic dreamer to be remembered for a handful of fanciful speeches. That may be the Martin Luther King that the world wishes to remember, but it is not the Martin Luther King that I have come to better understand and love even more.

The King that moves me most is the man who, during the final season of his earthly journey, faced a torrent of vicious assaults from virtually every segment of society, most painfully from his own people.

The symmetry is remarkable:

On April 4, 1967, he comes to the Riverside Church in New York City and delivers a dramatic and controversial speech in impassioned opposition to the Vietnam War.

Exactly twelve months later to the day, on April 4, 1968, he is assassinated in Memphis, where he has traveled on behalf of garbage workers.

The question I attempt to answer in this book is simple:

In his last year, what kind of man has Martin Luther King Jr. become?

In my view, he is a man whose true character has been misinterpreted, ignored, or forgotten. I want to remember— and bring to life—the essential truths about King in his final months before they are unremembered and irrecoverable. This is the King that I cherish: the King who, enduring a living hell, rises to moral greatness; the King who, in the face of unrelenting adversity, expresses the full measure of his character and courage. This is the King who, despite everything, spoke his truth, the man I consider the greatest public figure this country has ever produced.

In constructing this chronicle, I've conducted a series

of fresh interviews with three distinct groups: scholars, including his major biographers Taylor Branch, David Garrow, and Clayborne Carson; close friends like Harry Belafonte and Gardner C. Taylor; and associates including Andrew Young, Jesse Jackson, Dorothy Cotton, and Clarence Jones, among others. The insights gleaned from these firsthand observations have convinced me that the final leg of King's journey was far rougher than I had imagined. The pressures he faced were crushing. Yet he never compromised his core commitment to nonviolence. Not for a minute did he diminish his efforts to address the burning issues of racism, poverty, and the inherent immorality of this nation's unchecked militarism.

Nearly fifty years after King's death, these issues are more pressing than ever. And if, as we relive these last excruciating months in his life, we are made to understand that his mission remains unfulfilled—that the causes for which he gave his life continue to demand the immediate attention of our hearts and minds—then the purpose of this text will be fulfilled.

One final note about the tone of this text:

You will see that I attempt to convey King's inner thoughts during rare moments of self-reflection. Because he was a man in constant motion, these quiet, precious moments were few. My interpretation of these moments— my reading of what was on his mind—derives from my conversations with associates who were actually with him during those intimate times and privileged to hear him voice his heart.

You will also see that I refer to King as "Doc." This was how his most trusted colleagues addressed him. In adopting this nomenclature, I trust that I am not being presumptuous. I use this term of endearment as a way to bring me—and you—closer to the soul of the man.

*Tavis Smiley*
*Los Angeles, California*

# PART I

## FOUR SEASONS

*Spring, Summer, Fall, and Winter*

## Chapter One

# "VOCATION OF AGONY"

On Tuesday, April 4, 1967, Doc sits in his suite at the Americana Hotel in midtown Manhattan, realizing that everything about his public life is about to change. The moment of truth—Doc's truth—has arrived. An hour from now, when he stands in the pulpit of the august Riverside Church, he will face a congregation of four thousand people prepared to hang on his every word.

His mind is made up. He knows what he has to do. But his conviction, no matter how deep, cannot drown out the dissenting voices that clamor inside his head. These voices are more than mere phantoms. They reflect the views of the majority of his supporters. These voices, though now silent assaults, were once spoken aloud with feverish certainty.

*Stay in your lane.*

*You're a preacher, not a politician.*

*Don't overstep your bounds.*

*Don't overplay your hand.*

*You helped push through two of the most important pieces of legislation in our history—for civil and voting rights. Only a fool would now oppose the president who so aggressively championed our cause.*

*Attacking the Vietnam War is tantamount to attacking Lyndon Johnson. Why turn our most powerful ally into an enemy?*

*Why undermine the very movement to which you've devoted your life?*

*Why venture into an area—international politics— about which you have little or no expertise?*

*Why run the risk?*

*You're a Nobel laureate, a man respected the world over for his views on matters concerning minority rights and minority dignity. Why undermine your own dignity and standing—your exalted position as a leader of your people—by moving into the morass of arguments over a war that's irrelevant to your purpose?*

*Why destroy the hard-fought progress you have already made?*

*Your ego has run amok.*

*Your sense of restraint has abandoned you.*

*Where's your common sense?*

*Where's your concern for your supporters?*

*Why are you injuring them?*

*Why are you injuring yourself?*

The voices are persistent. Their ominous tone reflects the grave doubts of one of his most trusted aides and chief fund-raiser, Stanley Levison, who openly opposes the speech Doc is about to deliver.

Doc thinks back to the first draft of the speech written by Clarence Jones, a brilliant young black lawyer whom he recruited to the Southern Christian Leadership Conference in 1960. Jones had been reluctant to leave his Pasadena, California, home and promising corporate legal career. Even the fact that Doc had come to Jones's home on a Saturday night to personally persuade him didn't move the attorney. But come Sunday morning, sitting in the first pew of the Mt. Sinai Missionary Baptist Church and listening to King, as guest preacher, masterfully skewer the black middle class for refusing to fight for its own people, Jones surrendered to the preacher's call to action. The lawyer left his old life behind and became a tireless supporter. It was Jones, in fact, who visited Doc during the spring of 1963 when he was incarcerated in Alabama, where he had written in the margins of newspapers and small scraps of paper "Letter from Birmingham Jail," his celebrated defense of nonviolence.

"We should never forget that everything Adolf Hitler did in Germany was 'legal,'" wrote King, "...[and] it was 'illegal' to aid and comfort a Jew in Hitler's Germany. Even so, I am sure that, had I lived in Germany at the time, I would have aided and comforted my Jewish brothers. If today I lived in a Communist country where certain principles dear to the Christian faith are suppressed, I would openly advocate disobeying that country's antireligious laws."

Clarence Jones was dear to Doc's heart, but Jones's first draft of this Vietnam speech was too restrained, too balanced, too reflective of the lawyer's sense of moderation. King had come out against the war on previous occasions, but there had yet to be a definitive statement. So when the national conference of the Clergy and Laymen Concerned about Vietnam asked him to deliver its keynote address at Riverside, he quickly accepted.

As a man who has skillfully sought media attention to bring his message home, Doc understands the power of today's platform.

Riding in the back of the car as it winds its way through the city's swarming streets, he remembers a few months back, when, flipping through a magazine at an airport restaurant, he stopped at a photograph showing the horrific effects of napalm attacks on Vietnamese children.

His aide, seeing that he was no longer eating the food, said, "Doc, doesn't it taste any good?"

"Nothing will ever taste any good for me until I do everything I can to end that war."

In recent weeks Doc has twice canceled meetings with the world's most powerful man, Lyndon Johnson, whose civil rights support he had long courted and secured. Like all mortals, Doc is impressed by a White House invitation. But deeper wisdom tells him to avoid an encounter with a politician whose powers of persuasion are legendary. No doubt LBJ wants to get Doc to tone down his statements on the war when, in fact, Doc is about to dramatically turn up the volume.

It was only sixteen months ago—in January of 1966—that Doc had sent the president a telegram endorsing LBJ's peace efforts and his "reassuring" commitment to keep Vietnam from impeding progress in civil rights. But since the conflict has escalated alarmingly, Doc has come to view Johnson's win-at-all-costs policy as a catastrophe. Right now the last thing he needs is a one-on-one arm-twisting session with LBJ.

Martin Luther King is probably the only Negro in America prepared to turn down a private meeting with the president. It's not that his ego isn't excited by the prospect. Doc is a fiery preacher, and fiery preachers have strong egos. He likes recognition. He likes adulation. Yet his moral mission trumps his hunger for personal glory. He avoids Johnson because he does not want to be played by Johnson. His moral mission cannot be compromised.

The prepared text that he carries in his briefcase is largely the work of Vincent Harding—Korean War veteran, Mennonite peace activist, chairman of the history department at Spelman College, and Doc's Atlanta neighbor. It is a speech that, while setting out a compelling pro-peace position on high moral ground, carefully delineates the modern history of war-torn Vietnam.

As Doc arrives at 120th Street and Riverside Drive and looks out at the great Gothic edifice, his mind goes to the ironies of the moment. He reflects on the proximity of this opulent church, built largely through the contributions of John D. Rockefeller Jr. to the nearby neighborhood of Harlem, where impoverished people struggle for mere subsistence. He thinks of Dr. Harry Emerson Fosdick, Riverside's founding minister and eloquent voice of liberal Christianity, who fearlessly denounced racism during the dark days of the thirties and forties. He also thinks that were he ever to leave his beloved home church of Ebenezer Baptist in Atlanta, where he and his father are co-pastors, it would only be to lead a great progressive congregation like Riverside.

Stepping from the car and walking to the main sanctuary, he considers the furor he is about to create. He remains resolute.

After a standing ovation, the applause quiets and Doc gets down to business, declaring, "I come to this magnificent house of worship tonight because my conscience leaves me no other choice."

He quotes the directive of the conference's executive committee: "A time comes when silence is betrayal."

"Some of us," he says, "who have already begun to break the silence of the night have found that the calling to speak is often a vocation of agony, but we must speak."

He speaks of his own past ambivalence.

"Over the past two years, as I have moved to break the betrayal of my own silences and to speak from the burnings of my own heart, as I have called for radical departures from the destruction of Vietnam, many persons have questioned me about the wisdom of my path.... When I hear them, though I often understand the source of their concern, I am nevertheless greatly saddened, for such questions mean that the inquirers have not really known me, my commitment or my calling....

"In the light of such tragic misunderstanding, I deem it of signal importance to try to state clearly...why I believe that the path from Dexter Avenue Baptist Church — the church in Montgomery, Alabama, where I began my pastorate — leads clearly to this sanctuary tonight."

Now Doc is off and running. He quickly links the war — indeed, the very forces of militarism — to racism and poverty. Blacks are fighting and dying at almost twice their proportion of the population. He points to the "cruel irony of watching Negro and white boys on TV screens as they kill and die together for a nation that has been unable to seat them together at the same schools." He speaks about the rioters who, in answer to his plea for nonviolence, question America's own unchecked violence in Vietnam.

"Their questions hit home," he says, "and I knew that I could never again raise my voice against the violence of the oppressed in the ghettos without having first spoken clearly to the greatest purveyor of violence in the world today — my own government."

*The greatest purveyor of violence in the world today.*

The phrase will send shock waves through the media.

Doc's full-frontal attack on the war is unequivocal. His five-point plan is clear: Stop bombing, issue a unilateral cease-fire, abandon all bases in Southeast Asia, negotiate with North Vietnam's National Liberation Front, and set a date for complete troop removal.

The war is immoral. The immorality of the war is married to the immorality of poverty and racism. America must turn from the mad pursuit of this war to the pursuit of its moral integrity. "A nation that continues year after year to spend more money on military defense than on programs of social uplift," he claims, "is approaching spiritual death."

Like the Old Testament prophets he has studied and loved so well, Doc is delivering a prophesy in the sternest possible terms. "We are confronted with the fierce urgency of now. . . . We still have a choice today: nonviolent coexistence or violent coannihilation."

Moving away from his prepared speech, Doc begins to improvise. True to his bedrock Baptist roots, he points to Amos 5:24, calling forth a sense of faith and hope inherent to his tradition. He invokes a time when "justice will roll down like waters, and righteousness like a mighty stream."

The church explodes with thunderous applause. Again, an impassioned and sustained standing ovation.

His speech concluded, Doc leaves the sanctuary.

And then the real fireworks begin.

## Chapter Two

# "BETRAYING THE CAUSE"

On the long flight from New York City to Los Angeles, Doc looks out over the cloud covering of dark gray. Not a glimmer of sunshine. Nursing his stiff drink—vodka and orange juice—he tries to fight back the tears, but the emotions are too strong. The tears flow.

Doc thought he was prepared for the press reaction to his speech, but he wasn't. He isn't. The tears wet his cheeks. The tears expose the pain in his heart. His heavy heart is wounded by what is far more than a negative response. There is a viciousness to the attacks that assaults not only his position but his character as well.

The attacks from the mainstream press are unrelenting:

"Dr. King's Error" is the title of the *New York Times* editorial. "The political strategy of uniting the peace movement and the civil rights movement could very well be disastrous for both causes," claims the paper before calling Doc's approach "wasteful and self-defeating....Linking these hard, complex problems will lead not to solutions but to deeper confusion."

The *Washington Post* is even more damning: Doc "has done a grave injury to those who are his natural allies... and...an even graver injury to himself. Many who have listened to him with respect will never again accord him the same confidence. He has diminished his usefulness to his cause, to his country, and to his people."

"King has gone off on a tangent," declares *Life* magazine. "Instead of providing a share of the leadership that the faltering civil rights movement so desperately needs...he introduces matters that have nothing to do with the legitimate battle for equal rights here in America...[and] comes close to betraying the cause for which he has worked so long."

Even more painful for Doc, though, are the attacks from the country's most prominent black citizens. The people he thinks will be most sympathetic to his argument become, in many cases, his fiercest antagonists.

Carl Rowan, perhaps the most prestigious African American journalist—a former United States ambassador and former director of the United States Information Agency— writes in his nationally syndicated column, later to be expanded upon in *Reader's Digest,* one of the country's most widely read magazines, "Negroes had, in fact, begun to grow uneasy about King. He no longer seemed to be the selfless leader of the 1950s. There was grumbling that his trips to jail looked like publicity stunts. Bayard Rustin, a chief planner of the great civil rights March on Washington in 1963, and himself a pacifist, pleaded in vain with King not to wade into the Vietnam controversy.

"Why did King reject the advice of his old civil rights colleagues? Some say it was a matter of ego—that he was convinced that since he is the most influential Negro in the United States, President Johnson would have to listen to *him* and alter U.S. policy in Vietnam. Others received a more sinister speculation that had been whispered around Capitol Hill and in the nation's newsrooms for more than two years—talk of communists influencing the actions and words of the young minister. This talk disturbed other civil rights leaders more than anything else.... King has alienated many of the Negro's friends and armed the Negro's foes, in both parties, by creating the impression that the Negro is disloyal. By urging Negroes not to respond to the draft or to fight in Vietnam, he has taken a tack that many Americans of all races consider irresponsible."

Rowan points to a damning Harris poll indicating that one in every two blacks in America considers King dead wrong on the war question. Another 27 percent reserve comment.

If Rowan's assault isn't enough, Doc has to deal with the dagger being wielded by Dr. Ralph Bunche, his fellow Nobel laureate and the first African American to receive the prize. Bunche is not only the United Nations Under-Secretary-General for Political Affairs, but also a board member for the National Association for the Advancement of Colored People (NAACP)—the oldest and largest civil rights organization in American history. A solid citizen of the black bourgeoisie himself, Doc is devastated when, some days later, a front-page *New York Times* story reports that Bunche supported an NAACP board position to "oppose the effort to merge the civil rights and peace movements" and had, in fact, "moved to toughen the language of the... resolution by denouncing the merger attempt as a 'serious tactical mistake.'... He added that Walter P. Reuther, president of the United Auto Workers union, another NAACP board member, had supported his proposal."

Attacks from black intellectuals and policy makers is one thing; attacks from the grassroots black press is quite another. It isn't enough for the *Pittsburgh Courier* to go after him on Vietnam; the paper questions the merits of his recent civil rights work:

"It has only been a few months since Dr. King's Southern Christian Leadership Conference abandoned the South to attack problems in the urban north. Chicago was selected for its initial assault and there is still debate over the relative merits of that program last summer. Some have credited Dr. King and his SCLC followers with the defeat of long-time supporter of liberal causes Paul Douglas in his bid for the U.S. Senate. Others say the efforts did little to aid the plight of Chicago's South and West Side Negroes whose problems are more complex than those of a rural community in a Dixie located state." In a final blow, the paper concludes that Doc "does not speak for all Negro America and besides he is tragically misleading them."

Doc puts down the papers.

A second vodka and orange juice.

Another long look out on the vast gray expanse of sky.

A deep sigh.

He closes his eyes, tries to sleep, but sleep won't come. He reaches into his briefcase and pulls out a copy of the speech that has caused all this fury. As he reads it over, he reflects on what has happened. He knows that it wasn't his best delivery. Like the Mississippi blues singer and the New Orleans jazz musician, Doc is a freewheeling improviser. His greatest oratory moments have been spontaneous and, in the very moment of delivery, informed by the spirit, not a prepared text. Riverside was a prepared text. Because the speech was part history lesson and part peace plan, Doc had been careful to make a step-by-step case. That meant mostly sticking to the words written on the page. The result was a formality that subdued his typically soulful, free style.

The Riverside speech was also one of the rare times that Doc's aides distributed the complete text to the press. Not even his celebrated "I Have a Dream" address, delivered four summers ago from the steps of the Lincoln Memorial, had been mimeographed and made available to reporters covering the massive rally. John F. Kennedy had refused to attend that march. Afraid that Doc would provoke a riot, the president watched the proceedings on television from the White House. He refused to stand shoulder to shoulder with King. Only when the rally proved peaceful did Kennedy invite Doc and his cohorts to 1600 Pennsylvania Avenue for a photo op.

Doc smiles at the memory of a friend telling him that

"I Have a Dream," like "A Change Is Gonna Come" for Sam Cooke, would surely be remembered as his greatest hit. There were indeed high moments in that address:

"There will be neither rest nor tranquility in America until the Negro is granted his citizenship rights. The whirlwinds of revolt will continue to shake the foundations of our nation until the bright days of justice emerge. And that is something that I must say to my people who stand on the worn threshold which leads into the palace of justice. In the process of gaining our rightful place we must not be guilty of wrongful deeds. Let us not seek to satisfy our thirst for freedom by drinking from the cup of bitterness and hatred....

"I have a dream that one day on the red hills of Georgia sons of former slaves and the sons of former slave-owners will be able to sit down together at the table of brotherhood. I have a dream that one day even the state of Mississippi, a state sweltering with the heat of injustice...will be transformed into an oasis of freedom and justice.

"I have a dream that my four little children will one day live in a nation where they will not be judged by the color of their skin but by the content of their character. I have a dream...I have a dream that one day in Alabama, with its vicious racists, with its governor having his lips dripping with the words of interposition and nullification, one day right there in Alabama little black boys and black girls will be able to join hands with little white boys and white girls as sisters and brothers.

"I have a dream today.... When we allow freedom to

ring—when we let it ring from every village and every hamlet, from every state and every city, we will be able to speed up that day when all of God's children, black men and white men, Jews and Gentiles, Protestants and Catholics, will be able to join hands and sing in the words of the old Negro spiritual, 'Free at last, free at last, thank God Almighty, we are free at last.'"

That was August 28, 1963. Three short months later, on November 22, President Kennedy was assassinated in Dallas. In the view of many, America's age of innocence—renewed in the aftermath of World War II, elongated during the relatively sleepy two-term presidency of Dwight Eisenhower, and recharged by the Camelot aura of the early sixties—ended with that shocking tragedy. Kennedy died the death of a martyr. And LBJ, his successor, used that martyrdom to push through long-overdue legal protections for minorities.

*Protect us by protecting LBJ,* Doc's Negro critics are now telling him.

*Don't bite the hand that feeds us.*

*Be smart.*

*Be practical.*

*Stay in your lane.*

But now Doc has pulled onto a completely different highway. "I Have a Dream"—a moving and brilliantly succinct sermon—was delivered at the right time in the right place, before a throng of a quarter million in the nation's capital. For all its biting critique of racist America, Doc's message was hardly viewed as controversial. Like a lyrical piece of popular music, it resonated with the great masses. It was, in fact, an enormous hit.

Now, according to the nation's most powerful opinion makers, Riverside is a colossal failure, a fatal mistake in the career of a man who has overstepped his bounds and lost his way.

*Why this sudden reversal?*

Doc finishes off his second vodka and reflects on the enormity of that question. To his mind, his "Beyond Vietnam" speech was a carefully constructed argument — logical, cogent, and irrefutable. He'd been told that the distribution of his remarks to the press that evening would help his case. Yet it had exactly the opposite effect.

As an astute observer of the American scene, Doc knew full well that the culture wars were escalating — young versus old, doves versus hawks. He knew that not everyone would be pleased when, with unapologetic defiance, he took on the Johnson administration. But he had no notion that the reaction to his remarks would be the most uniformly and viciously negative of a public career going back to the Montgomery Bus Boycott of 1955.

The vitriol behind those attacks has his head throbbing. The idea that he is "tragically misleading" his people is nothing he wants to consider. He wants to order a third drink but asks the stewardess to bring him a cup of coffee instead. He feels like having a cigarette. His policy is not to smoke in public, but the plane is half-empty and, with his aide sitting in the aisle seat next to him, Doc is afforded a privacy that allows him to light up a Salem. For much of his adult life he's vowed to quit smoking. Not long ago he even made the pledge to his wife, Coretta. But when she found a pack in his coat pocket, he did what men often do — he blamed it on someone else. He told Coretta the cigarettes belonged to Tom Houck, his driver. From then on, after being dropped off at night, Doc handed his Salems to Tom, only to get them back the next morning.

He draws on his smoke. Could he be "tragically misleading" his people? As a highly educated intellectual who believes in challenging one's own ideas, Doc has always been his sternest critic. And like all people of faith, he has to deal with his doubts.

He thinks back to how his doubts were excited by his encounters with Stanley Levison. A Jewish lawyer who has dedicated his life to the Southern Christian Leadership Conference, Levison works without pay. Doc never doubts Levison's devotion and especially values the fact that Levison, unlike some other aides, has no personal agenda or ambitions of his own. Levison's opinions cannot be ignored.

When it came to Riverside, Levison was forthright.

"I am afraid you will become identified as a leader of a fringe movement when you are much more," Levison said when he read the text that he also characterized as "unbalanced and poorly thought out." He further offered, "I do not think [the speech] was a good expression of you."

Doc, who relished a good debate, fought back, arguing that the speech might be "politically unwise but morally wise.... I really feel that someone of influence has to say that the United States is wrong, and everybody is afraid to say it.... I have just become so disgusted with the way people of America are being brainwashed...by the administration."

In the aftermath of the speech, though, Levison's cautionary words hit Doc hardest. Responding to King's hope that his speech would sway public opinion—and the administration—toward a withdrawal from Vietnam, the lawyer had said, "It will be harder than Birmingham."

Looking out the window of the plane, Doc sees that the clouds have parted. The sun is shining. The sky is a luminous blue. The captain announces that they are passing over the city of Chicago. The city Doc chose when, two years ago, he traveled north to champion the plight of the urban poor.

"In the South, we always had segregationists to help make issues clear," he said at the time. "This ghetto Negro has been invisible so long and has become visible through violence."

Rather than live in a hotel suite or a comfortable high-rise, Doc moved into the heart of the ghetto: a $90-a-week third-floor walk-up flat in the neighborhood of North Lawndale—nicknamed Slumdale—where he led the Chicago Freedom Movement, a multipronged assault on the brutal discrimination facing the underprivileged in housing, health, education, and employment. It was also in Chicago that Doc addressed the issue of urban violence and met face-to-face with the leaders of the city's most notorious gangs.

From the very start, Doc's efforts were bitterly opposed

by the formidable Chicago Democratic machine, led by Mayor Richard Daley, a Johnson ally—the same Daley who used his mighty influence in a calculated attempt to discredit Doc's campaign and obliterate his reputation. It was Daley who only last July warned LBJ that Doc is "not your friend. He's against you on Vietnam. He's a goddamn faker."

Doc's sworn enemies have, for some time now, been among the most powerful people in government, including J. Edgar Hoover, director of the FBI. As Doc wings his way west, he is fully aware that his opponents have been emboldened by his speech at Riverside; still, he has no idea that Hoover has not only planted spies among the upper echelon of the Southern Christian Leadership Conference, but has also set wiretaps to monitor the phone calls of Doc and his aides. One of the spies is James Harrison, the treasurer of SCLC, who, for nearly two years, has been taking under-the-table money from the FBI to report on the activities of Doc and his organization. Another is Ernest Withers, a black freelance photographer and an insider in the civil rights movement who has spent an enormous amount of time covering Doc all across the country.

Back in 1964, it was the FBI that anonymously mailed Doc a vicious letter from an assailant urging him to kill himself. Unfortunately, it was Coretta who opened the package. "King," it stated, "there is only one thing left for you to do. You know what this is. You have just 34 days in which to do (this exact number has been selected for a specific reason, it has definite practical significance). You are done. There is but one way out for you. You better take it before your filthy, abnormal fraudulent self is bared to the nation."

The letter accused him of grave moral improprieties along with a tape made by bugging Doc's hotel rooms. On the tape Doc is telling off-color jokes. There are also suggestions and sounds of sexual activity. But somehow his marriage has weathered the storm.

Another cup of coffee, another Salem, another long look out the window; the sky is again covered by clouds. The plane hits an air pocket. The captain warns of rough weather ahead. Doc straps on his seat belt. He is used to rough weather of every variety. He has been flying in and out of storms for the greater part of his life.

Some of those storms nearly took him out.

Back in 1958, he was at a book signing in Harlem when a woman plunged a knife in his chest.

Four years later, a white power fanatic in Birmingham jumped to the stage as Doc was speaking. The assailant hit Doc in the face, struck him on the side of the head and punched him in the gut. The preacher put up no resistance. He simply got up and, after the attacker was taken away, somehow completed his remarks.

During a march in Chicago to protest housing segregation, Doc faced a placard that read "King would look good with a knife in his back." During that same march a stone struck him on the head and felled him to his knees. To protect Doc from an onslaught of flying bottles, rocks, and firecrackers, his aides surrounded him, but the minister kept marching. Afterward he said, "I have to do this—to expose myself—to bring this hate into the open." Then he added, "I have seen many demonstrations in the South, but I have never seen anything so hostile and so hateful as I've seen here today."

That was last year in Chicago.

This year after Riverside, the hate and hostility, like the war in Vietnam that Doc so passionately opposes, will escalate to even higher and more dangerous levels.

His mood is sullen. The sheer number of attacks has taken its toll and wounded his spirit. But wounded or not, he summons the strength to start plotting out his plan for the rest of the year—more protests against America's rising militarism and, if God wills him to live long enough, the mobilization of a sweeping Poor People's Campaign that will transform the national conscience and spotlight the pressing needs of those who, in the words of the gospel of Matthew, are "the least of these my brothers and sisters."

The plane flies into the center of the storm. The turbulence is severe but not severe enough to keep Doc from reaching for his notebook and getting to work.

## Chapter Three

# "THE LANGUAGE OF THE UNHEARD"

Doc is a minister on the move. For the past decade he has lived life at a frenetic pace, crisscrossing the country in jets and puddle jumpers, on buses and in cars, accompanied by aides and advisers with whom he confers on the run. His days are jam-packed with phone calls, press conferences, speeches, and strategy sessions. He is a crusader in a tremendous hurry, a paradoxical symbol of a super activist-pacifist. His work ethos is beyond excessive. He is incapable of slowing down.

And yet in April of 1967, Doc faces a firewall of criticism that, at least for now, has him reeling. When his plane lands in Los Angeles, he hurries to an overcrowded press conference at the Biltmore Hotel. He is testy. Stanley Levison has written for him a defense of Riverside, an argument that the speech did not — as the news accounts have reported—call for a literal merger of the civil rights and peace movements. As a natural-born advocate, Doc does not relish being on the defensive. Furthermore, he does not want to give the appearance of backing down from his antiwar position. When it comes to sparring matches with the press, he is an old pro, a nimble opponent and skilled debater. But today in California, sensing his weariness and vulnerability, the reporters are unrelenting. Question after question comes down to the same charge:

*Isn't your Riverside speech injuring your own cause and your own people?*

Tired of the assault, Doc fires back at the press: "The war in Vietnam is a much greater injustice to Negroes than anything I could say against that war."

From Los Angeles Doc flies to San Francisco and on Friday, April 14, is driven to Stanford University in Palo Alto, where he's set to give another speech. During phone calls to New York and Atlanta, he is in continual consultation with his advisers, who are now warning him about the danger of his appearing at still another pivotal event, this one to unfold back in New York City the very next day.

A massive assembly of antiwar protestors will march from Central Park to the United Nations. Called The Mobilization, the rally will surely ratchet up the impassioned positions—pro and con—concerning Vietnam. The media will treat it as headline news.

Doc is slated to speak. Now his advisers are urging him not to. Their most critical concern is that Doc's appearance will link him to the radical left, thus undermining his credibility with more moderate liberals, the source of the civil rights movement's strength. Again, it's Stanley Levison who warns Doc that the press will further excoriate him for associating with extremists, especially Stokely Carmichael, the face of the rising black militancy and a man for whom Black Power has turned into a battle cry—a chant that is exciting black youth and alienating King's white supporters.

But even before Doc deals with Stokely, how does he address the more militant segment of his own movement? The brilliant but wildly unpredictable James Bevel, Doc's own director of education for SCLC as well as one of the architects of the March on Washington and the Selma-to-Montgomery march, has talked about coming to The Mobilization with a group of Sioux Indians. Bevel wants to demonstrate against the United States' original sin—the genocide of Native Americans.

In an urgent call to Doc from Rabbi Abraham Joshua Heschel, a noted professor-philosopher and another close ally, the clergyman is claiming that Bevel's demonstration will serve only to radicalize the march, causing Doc further damage.

Though Doc and Bevel are both Southern Baptist preachers, the two men are a contrast in styles: Doc is the conservative coat-and-tie dresser, while Bevel wears funky farmer's overalls and, on his shaved head, a yarmulke, the skullcap of observant Jews, in tribute to the Old Testament prophets.

Back in January, Doc was in Jamaica working on his

new book when Bevel unexpectedly appeared. Doc has always held deep affection for James. Their Christian bond is strong. And though Doc has long benefited from Bevel's visionary thinking, he also knows that James is something of a firebrand whose impetuosity is not always productive. James's arrival came at a propitious time: Doc was still formulating his Vietnam position. Riverside was four months away.

It was in Jamaica that Bevel asked the question for which Doc had no easy answer: Why was he "teaching non-violence to Negroes in Mississippi, but not to Lyndon Johnson in Vietnam? Are the Vietnamese not your brothers and sisters?"

That was winter. Now in spring Doc has embraced Bevel's unequivocal antiwar stance. He still gives consideration to his other advisers' characterization of Bevel as a lunatic "over-simplifier," but of greater concern is Carmichael, head of SNCC, the Student Nonviolent Coordinating Committee, an organization that is quickly — and ironically — becoming disenchanted with the premise of nonviolence.

As spring turns to summer, Stokely's status is rising as Doc's is falling. Stokely is brimming with fresh charisma. Doc is tired. Stokely is angry black America's warrior prince. Doc is the older generation's portly preacher. Lean and tall, with burning dark eyes and chiseled facial features, Stokely is twenty-five; Doc is thirty-eight. The incendiary tone of Stokely's oratory triggers the volatile restlessness of the counterculture sixties. In this increasingly violent decade, his call to arms resonates. Doc's defense of nonviolence, with its historical roots in Mahatma Gandhi's 1920s pacifism, seems to have lost steam and struggles for relevance.

Doc has delivered his speech at Stanford. Now he faces another decision: Should he or should he not race up to the San Francisco airport and catch the late-night flight to New York? Given Doc's state of mind, canceling his appearance at another mega-media antiwar event makes good common sense. With both the press and his advisers on his back, why not skip it, remain in California, get a good night's sleep, and go home to Atlanta for a day or two of much-needed rest?

It's 8 a.m. when the red-eye touches down on the runway at New York's Kennedy Airport, so renamed only four years prior. Doc awakens with a startle. With just a few hours' sleep behind him, he is driven into Manhattan and rushed through the throng of waiting marchers to The Mobilization's meeting point in Central Park, where he is escorted to the front line. His great friend Harry Belafonte is waiting for him. The men embrace.

Of all of Doc's celebrity supporters, Belafonte is by far the most serious. In the fifties, dubbed the "King of Calypso," he became one of America's biggest pop stars as both a singer and an actor. He joined up with Doc during the Montgomery Bus Boycott and has remained close to him ever since. Recently, he has dedicated far more time to his role as social activist than entertainer.

Doc and Harry are joined by Dr. Benjamin Spock, another activist as well as a renowned pediatrician, and Dave Dellinger, a radical who visited South and North Vietnam in 1966 and returned with a firsthand report on the catastrophic impact of the American bombing. Stokely Carmichael emerges from the crowd, shakes Doc's hand, and takes his place with the others in the front rank.

Before the march starts, several police officials take Doc aside to report a rash of assassination threats. There is talk of snipers. The cops make it clear that there is simply no way to guarantee King's safety. It's another chance for the minister to withdraw.

Doc has been threatened before. He'll be threatened again. He's learned to live with the feeling of extreme vulnerability. He stuffs the fear in his back pocket and rejoins his fellow protestors.

In the spring before the Summer of Love, there is already a large constituency of hippies cropping up in the mass protest movements in the country's major cities. Today in New York is no different. Young women in tie-dyed granny dresses and their long-haired boyfriends mingle with professors, physicians, and other professionals, plus scores of everyday people—garment workers, secretaries, sales clerks—fed up with a war policy that they can no longer accept or tolerate. The protestors feel empowered by their sheer number. Comprising a twenty-block procession, they are 125,000.

Before the march begins, there is a ceremony that the news media eagerly photographs and films: as the crowd cheers wildly, seventy Cornell students light matches to their draft cards.

This is the era of brutal confrontation. The hippies and peaceniks excite violent animosity. Their detractors are out in force. Along the way the marchers are splattered with paint. When they pass a construction site, the hard hats pelt them with nails. It takes four hours to reach the United Nations.

Before Doc goes to the podium to deliver a speech, an abbreviation of his Riverside remarks, he glances up at the United Nations headquarters and, for a fleeting second, thinks of Nobel laureate Ralph Bunche, whose offices are on the thirty-fourth floor of this very building. Back in California, Doc had called Bunche, hoping to reconcile the growing differences between them. The conversation was less than satisfying. Doc complained to his aides that Bunche had been maddeningly evasive.

The assemblage cannot help but contrast Doc's speech with Stokely's. Doc concludes his remarks with a plea to stop the bombing. But Carmichael is more dramatic and dynamic.

"When we look at the America which brought slaves here once in ships named Jesus, we charge genocide. When we look at the America which seized land from Mexico and practically destroyed the American Indians—we charge genocide. When we look at all the acts of racist exploitation which this nation has committed, whether in the name of manifest destiny or anti-Communism, we charge genocide....

"There is an almost endless list of these other Americas, but they all add up to the same thing: this nation was built on genocide and it continues to wage genocide. It wages genocide in many forms—military, political, economic and cultural—against the colored peoples of our earth. This nation has been not only anti-revolutionary but anti-poor, anti-wretched of the earth....

"This nation's hypocrisy has no limits. Newspapermen speak of LBJ's credibility gap; I call it lying. President Lyndon Baines Johnson talks of peace while napalming Vietnamese children, and I can think of just one thing: he's talking trash out of season, without a reason. Let's not call it anything but that.

"It is up to you—to the people here today—to make your fellow citizens see this other side of America. In your great numbers lies a small hope. But this mass protest must not end here. We must move from words to deeds. We must go back to our communities and organize against the war. Black people must begin to organize the ghettoes for control by the people and against exploitation. Exploitation and racism do not exist only in this nation's foreign policy, but right here in the streets of New York."

Bringing it home to the hot-button issue being played up by the press—today's destruction of draft cards—Stokely reaches a fever pitch. "The draft," he shouts, "is white people sending black people to make war on yellow people in order to defend the land they stole from red people. The draft must end: not tomorrow, not next week, but today."

When Stokely quotes the black poet Margaret Walker—"Let another world be born. Let a second generation full of courage issue forth....Let the martial songs be written, let the dirges disappear. Let a race of men now rise and take control!"—he is clearly not referring to men who belong to the generation of Martin Luther King Jr.

That night in Belafonte's Manhattan apartment, Doc and the others stay up till the wee hours of the morning analyzing the day's events. Doc is gratified that the turnout was enormous, the biggest antiwar rally in the history of New York City. He is convinced that the enormity of The Mobilization exceeded that of the 1963 March on Washington. Some of his supporters feel that Stokely was condescending to Doc. Others, like Belafonte, are obviously taken with the young leader's fiery rhetoric.

If you asked the FBI agents what they heard, since they'd been listening in all the while via a wiretapped call, they might tell you that Levison is worried that Belafonte will move into Stokely's camp. But Doc is certain that the entertainer will not abandon the cause of nonviolence—his cause.

Still sleep deprived, Doc is up early on Sunday morning for an appearance on CBS's *Face the Nation*, on which a panel of journalists, especially eager to break him down, grill him for thirty minutes.

"Dr. King, yesterday you led a demonstration here which visibly featured the carrying of Vietcong flags, a mass burning of drafts cards and one American flag was burned.... How far should this go?"

Without compromising his staunch antiwar position, Doc carefully separates himself from draft card burners and Vietcong flag-wavers. At the same time, he states that if he were facing the draft, "I myself would be a conscientious objector."

When asked why he would share a platform with a radical like Carmichael, Doc answers that he recently appeared in Nashville with segregationist senator Strom Thurmond. "I don't think you have to agree with someone politically and philosophically in order to appear on the same platform."

Displaying his usual aplomb, Doc doesn't sidestep the questions but deftly manages to make larger points. "The Great Society," he says, "with its very noble programs, in a sense has been shot down on the battlefields of Vietnam."

When asked about the white backlash against the rising black militancy, he says, "It may well be that Black Power and riots are the consequence of the white backlash rather than the cause of them.... In the final analysis a riot is the language of the unheard. And what is it that America has failed to hear—it has failed to hear that the plight of the Negro poor has worsened over the last twenty years, that the promises of justice and equality have not been met, and that large segments of white society are more concerned about tranquility and the status quo than about justice and humanity. This, to me, is the white backlash."

Later that day, when reporters ask about talk of a Martin Luther King candidacy for the presidency — with Dr. Benjamin Spock as his running mate — Doc denies any interest in mounting such a campaign.

Throughout April, the talk doesn't go away. Spock himself wants Doc to make the run. The White House is so concerned that it contacts King aide Andrew Young to see if Doc will agree to see the president.

Doc is interested in neither meeting with the president nor becoming the president. He continues to disavow any presidential ambitions, telling this to Spock himself when the two men meet in Cambridge to announce their plans for a "Vietnam Summer," a national volunteer movement to mobilize opposition.

Doc's mantra doesn't change: he's a preacher, not a politician.

He's a preacher who, in his own words, "lives out of a suitcase and needs only four hours sleep a night," a preacher who must continually fight back the demons of despondency as the challenges facing his ministry grow greater. To meet those challenges, he does what preachers do: he preaches.

For all his hyperactive work as a social justice spokesman and political reformer, Doc is essentially a clergyman. Every Sunday that he can, he comes home to minister in the pulpit of his church, Ebenezer Baptist. It is the church where his father has preached for decades. It is neither the largest nor the most prestigious church in the city. It is a respectable but in most ways ordinary church situated in the middle-class black community of Atlanta.

The church is Doc's anchor. It is where he returns to reflect on the state of his soul. In the middle of his tumultuous public life, the church provides him with great solace. In the sermons he preaches at Ebenezer, we see not only a man who is speaking to his congregation but a man who is speaking to God, a man seeking spiritual energy to drive him forward.

## Chapter Four

# "ANXIETY AND SORROW IN MY HEART"

For Doc, the route back home to Ebenezer is always circuitous. The demands on his time—like the demands from conscience—never cease.

He stops off in Cleveland to meet with the United Pastors Association, a group of black ministers, who are worried about the upcoming summer. A year ago there were riots in the Hough ghetto. Seeking Doc's advice, the preachers want to avoid another violent insurgence. Before leaving town, Doc lends his support to Carl Stokes, who, in the fall, has a chance to become the first black elected mayor of a major American city.

On his way back to the airport, Doc remembers another trip to Cleveland, when aide Bernard Lee was driving him and Andy Young down Euclid Avenue. Doc was scheduled to deliver a sermon at the Olivet Institutional Baptist Church, pastored by his dear friend and fellow Morehouse man Otis Moss. When the car stopped at a red light, a group of young black prostitutes recognized Doc and began taunting him.

"There's that old Uncle Tom."

"Why don't you just go back to Georgia?"

As Bernard drove on, Doc was still trying to process the sneers. A few seconds later, he told Bernard to turn the car around.

"What for?" asked Andy.

"I need to talk to those girls. I need to explain."

"Look, Doc," said Andy. "We don't have time. We'll be late to church."

Doc was unmoved. Church will wait. "Bernard," he repeated, "turn this car around."

When they had driven back up to the women, Doc got out of the car. He explained that he could understand their feelings about him. At the same time, he wanted to clarify what he was trying to accomplish. He didn't have time to go into it now, but would they do him the courtesy of meeting him later that afternoon at his hotel, where, over a cup of coffee, they could all have a chance to speak openly? Surprised, the women agreed.

At 4 p.m., more than a dozen women in miniskirts and short shorts marched into the Sheraton, went up to the reception desk, and asked to see Dr. Martin Luther King Jr. Taken aback, the clerk wasn't sure what to do.

"Just call up to his room," said one of the women. "We're his guests. You'll see."

The clerk made the call and Doc arranged to meet them in the hotel's conference room, where coffee, sandwiches, and sweets were served. He thanked the women for coming and let them know that he was interested in hearing their points of view.

The women were hardly reticent. They explained how they related much more to the late Malcolm X than to King. A former hustler, Malcolm knew the streets; he understood their harsh reality; he'd been in touch with the brutal struggles of black folks. His response to those struggles was aggressive—not passive, like Doc's.

Rather than defend himself, Doc let the women go on telling their stories. A few of them were still teenagers; others were in their early twenties. He thought of the abject conditions of ghetto life that force females to sell their bodies. He thought of the terrible pain ensuing from the destruction of innocence.

Lives demolished by neglect.

Though it was a completely different context, perhaps Doc thought of the four innocent girls—three of whom were young teenagers—killed in the 1963 bombing of the 16th Street Baptist Church in Birmingham, Alabama, the same church where Doc and his supporters had often met.

Lives ended by hatred.

All lives precious in God's sight.

The women had much to say, and Doc carefully considered their words. When they were through, he briefly tried to explain himself. He was a preacher who espoused the Christian gospel of love. His job was to love, not to judge. He spoke of the abysmal social and economic conditions that plagued black America. He described these as desperate times. He also explained why he still clung to his belief in nonviolence. In his view, nonviolence not only ultimately produces positive change but protects the peaceful integrity of our very souls.

The women may or may not have agreed. But they were moved by the fact that this famous minister had taken the time to hear them out—and had taken them seriously. He said that no matter where we may be in our life's journey, we are all children of God. That statement touched their hearts.

After the women left, Doc returned to his reflection on the death of innocence. His mind drifted back to the darkest of days in Birmingham, when he had delivered the eulogy at the funeral of the girls, who, before the detonation of the bomb, were on their way to a Sunday school lesson called "The Love That Forgives." It was then that he said, "Life is hard, at times as hard as crucible steel. It has its bleak and difficult moments. Like the ever-flowing waters of the river, life has its moments of drought and its moments of flood....If one will hold on, he will discover that God walks with him....God is able to lift you from the fatigue of despair to the buoyancy of hope, and transform dark and desolate valleys into sunlit paths of inner peace."

That eulogy was one of the few times Doc was ever seen weeping openly in public.

\* \* \*

A few days after Cleveland, there is no peace in Louisville, the hometown of Muhammad Ali. In national news, there is word that, in retaliation for the boxer's refusal to be drafted, the World Boxing Association is on the verge of summarily stripping the champ of his championship belt.

Doc has come to Louisville to join forces with his baby brother, A. D.—the minister at the local Zion Baptist Church—in a march protesting the city's racist housing practices. Four hundred people join the ministers, who face a bevy of angry hecklers. Rocks hurled by the haters strike both Doc and A. D. The wounds are not critical. Retaliation is not an option. The brothers march on.

Later that day the news about Ali is confirmed: his antiwar stance has gotten him banned from boxing. A. D. remembers how only a month ago, during the SCLC board meeting right here in Louisville, Doc excused himself from a strategy session and slipped away to a private meeting with Ali.

The two men—the Baptist pacifist preacher and the Muslim heavyweight brawler—understand each other on the deepest level. Both charismatic stars, they are continually pursued by willing women wherever they travel. But each is also a serious thinker who addresses the issue of racism in a unique way. Despite Ali's close association with Malcolm X, he sees King as a fighter for the cause of justice. Doc applauds Ali's brave opposition to the war. He has been moved by Ali's commonsense statement widely embraced by the black community: "You keep asking me, no matter how long, about the war in Vietnam, I sing this song. I ain't got no quarrel with the Vietcong. Ain't no Vietcong ever called me nigger."

"He is giving up even fame," Doc would later say in support of the champ. "He is giving up millions of dollars in order to stand up for what his conscience tells him is right.... There is a very dangerous development in the nation now to equate dissent with disloyalty."

While Doc's public work is all about peaceful dissent, disloyalty to his wife, Coretta, brings heavy guilt to his heart. It is, for instance, after meeting with Ali and concluding the SCLC board meeting in Louisville that Doc begins what Georgia Davis, a woman who will soon be elected the first black state senator in Kentucky, would claim decades later to be an affair with her.

Back in Atlanta on the last Sunday in April, Doc uses his sermon to sort out his feelings. He wants his church to understand this uproar over his antiwar position. He implores Stokely Carmichael, who happens to be in the city, to attend the morning service at Ebenezer. At the Mobilization rally in New York, Stokely was clearly the star. Now here in his home church, playing on his home court, Doc is eager for the young radical to hear him at his very best. Doc feels an urgent need to gain Stokely's allegiance.

"They applauded us when we non-violently decided to sit in at lunch counters," Doc preaches. "They applauded us on the Freedom Rides when we accepted blows without retaliation. They praised us in Albany and Birmingham and Selma....Oh, the press was so noble in its applause, so noble in its praise when I was saying be non-violent toward Bull Connor.... There's something strangely inconsistent about a nation and a press that will praise you when you say, 'Be non-violent toward [segregationist sheriff] Jim Clark,' but will curse you and damn you when you say, 'Be non-violent toward little brown Vietnamese children.' There's something wrong with the press."

Doc doesn't go long without mentioning "the ministry of Jesus Christ. To me, the relationship of this ministry to the making of peace is so obvious that I sometimes marvel at those who ask me why I am speaking out against the war. Could it be that they do not know that the Good News was meant for all men, for communists and capitalists, for their children and ours, for black and white, for revolutionary and conservative? Have they forgotten that my ministry is in obedience to the One who loved His enemies so fully that he died for them? What, then, can I say to the Vietcong, or to Castro, or to Mao, as a faithful minister to Jesus Christ? Can I threaten them with death, or must I not share with them my life? Finally, I must be true to my conviction that I share with all men, the calling to be the son of the Living God. Beyond the calling of race or nation or creed is this vocation of sonship and brotherhood. And because I believe the Father is deeply concerned, especially for His suffering and helpless and outcast children, I come today to speak for them."

A little later in the sermon, looking directly at Carmichael, Doc becomes more pointedly political.

"Oh, my friends," he preaches, "if there is any one thing that we must see today it is that these are revolutionary times. All over the globe men are revolting against old systems of exploitation and oppression, and out of the wounds of a frail world, new systems of justice and equality are being born. The shirtless and barefoot people are rising up as never before....

"I speak out against this war, not in anger, but with anxiety and sorrow in my heart, and, above all, with a passionate desire to see our beloved country stand as a moral example of the world."

At the end of the sermon, Stokely is among those who rise to give the preacher a standing ovation.

Doc wonders whether he has really won over Carmichael and the impatient black youth whom Carmichael represents. He wonders whether he has even won over the confidence of his own organization, increasingly critical of his every move.

No matter: it is good to be home, good to be together with Coretta and his young children, Yolanda, Martin III, Dexter, and Bernice, good to preach at Ebenezer before those who know and love him best. Among his beloved congregation, the goodwill is strong.

But the goodwill does not transfer to other settings, or other cities. In the venomous climate of America in 1967, goodwill is one thing that does not last long.

## Chapter Five

# THE BLOODIEST MONTH OF ALL

It's the third week of May and the weather has turned warm in Savannah, Georgia. Doc lets out a long sigh as he walks off the plane. It's been a hellacious winter and spring. He welcomes this early taste of summer's heat. He also welcomes the idea of being whisked off to South Carolina's St. Helena Island, a retreat that affords him an opportunity to relax. And yet the prospect of meeting with the entire staff of SCLC — some seventy members strong — is far from relaxing. The organization is at war with itself. More than at any other time in SCLC history, the rank and file are emboldened to question Doc's leadership. Just as firebrand radicals like Carmichael are upstaging Doc from outside SCLC, there are young leaders inside the group who represent the same kind of generational divide.

Jesse Jackson, for example, is the tall, dashing, twenty-five-year-old former football hero turned minister turned rising star. Having taken over Operation Breadbasket in Chicago—a branch of SCLC that focuses on economic equity in the urban ghettoes—Jackson appeals to youth in a way that Doc does not. Even Doc's staunchest supporters are beginning to whisper among themselves that if anyone can compete with the Black Power advocates for the heart and soul of the black community, it's going to be a charismatic figure like Jesse, not Doc.

For now, though, Doc puts away those thoughts. He greets Tom Barnwell, who has come to the airport to drive him to St. Helena Island, an hour up the coast.

"Loosen your tie, Doc," says Tom, "and enjoy the ride."

The most formal of men, Doc rarely removes his coat and tie, but St. Helena is one spot where he can loosen up. St. Helena is a lush sea island, a casual-clothes-only kind of place. Free from the pressure of reporters or photographers, Doc can stroll the forty acres of the Penn Center, the grounds of one of the earliest schools for freed slaves and the location of the SCLC conference. Penn is also one of the few settings in the Deep South where interracial conclaves have been conducted without hassle. It is a bucolic sanctuary, a place apart.

Driving up Highway 21, Tom relishes this time alone with Doc. A man who speaks his mind, Tom wants to talk economics. He initiates a conversation about his concern that SCLC's focus on boycotting businesses refusing to recirculate money back into black neighborhoods could negatively impact black employees of those very businesses. Brothers and sisters could lose their jobs.

Although Doc usually enjoys a lively intellectual exchange, this time he resists. With the window rolled down and fresh air blowing in, he'd rather relax, have a smoke, and save the heavy discussions till later.

"No, Brother Barnwell," is all he says, "the Lord will provide."

Sensing that Doc isn't in a talkative mood, Tom asks whether he'd like to listen to the radio. Of course. When Tom explains that there may not be gospel music at this time of day, Doc assures him that there's nothing wrong with a little rhythm and blues. Tom slides the dial to a station that's playing the opening strains of "When Something Is Wrong with My Baby," the current hit by Sam and Dave, one of Doc's favorites.

A fan of the deep-fried Southern soul coming off Memphis's Stax record label, Doc lets his mind slide back to a few months earlier, when, on an off night in New York, he slipped into Madison Square Garden to see Ike and Tina Turner open for Sam and Dave. The memory brings a smile to his lips. Tina sang and shimmied with such sensuous sway that the crowd wouldn't stop calling her name — "Tina! Tina! Tina!" — even after she had exited the stage and Sam and Dave had come on. The Dynamic Duo, as Sam and Dave were billed, finally won over the fans, but only after removing their jackets and shirts. Doc loved the show from start to finish. Along with the rest of the crowd, he got his groove on. He felt renewed. Backstage, he congratulated the guys, acknowledging the herculean effort it had taken, after Tina's triumph, to recapture the musical momentum. He took the opportunity to ask Sam and Dave to join him on an SCLC fund-raising tour he is planning for this summer. The guys unhesitatingly agreed. So had Aretha Franklin, Tony Bennett, Harry Belafonte, and the Staple Singers.

As the Sam and Dave song fades, Doc thinks ahead to the tour. Given SCLC's precarious finances, it's critical that the concerts are successful.

"I found a gospel station, Doc," says Tom Barnwell. "This should make you happy."

It does. It's an old Mahalia Jackson hymn from way back when—"In the Upper Room." The story is about dwelling in the upper room with Jesus, trusting his grace and power, seeking his love in prayer. The enormous richness of her voice stirs Doc mightily. He struggles to keep from crying— not for sadness but for the melodic majesty of God's glory. Doc is close not only to the song but to the singer herself. He calls his friend "Halie." The only woman at the podium during the March on Washington, Halie, the consummate performer, was the one who realized on that monumental day that Doc's oration was at one point beginning to lag.

"Tell 'em about the dream, Doc," Halie urged King, having heard him employ the catchphrase in earlier speeches. "Tell 'em about the dream."

When Doc took her cue and began reciting the "I have

a dream" refrain, Halie broke into a wide smile. The day was won.

This day in South Carolina is being brightened by the music from Tom Barnwell's radio. Soul music, whether secular or sacred, energizes Doc's spirit. The low-country landscape soothes his eyes as the sound of another gospel favorite, the Caravans' "Mary, Don't You Weep," soothes his ears. While there is no reason to weep, there is good reason to gird himself for a conference that will be anything but soothing.

In a small cottage on the edge of the Penn Center campus in St. Helena Island's Frogmore community, Doc awakes after a restless night. The full staff is waiting for him in the main meeting room. He walks through the marshy terrain at a brisk pace, hoping that the daytime portion of the conference will adjourn while there is still enough light for a softball game.

He thinks back on the recent tensions and sharp divisions inside SCLC, an organization that is more fractious than ever. His top-ranking lieutenant and closest friend, Ralph Abernathy, a fellow Baptist preacher and the man with whom Doc began the Montgomery Bus Boycott back in the winter of '55, has been demonstrably discontent since traveling to Sweden for the Nobel Peace Prize ceremony in the winter of '64. Outside the hotel, the honor guard arrived in a grand state car to drive the party to the ceremony at the University of Oslo. Doc and Coretta got in the car, but when Abernathy made a move to join them, he was abruptly stopped. Ralph protested, explaining that, along with Doc, he was a coleader of the movement. The guard was unmoved. No entrée for Ralph. Abernathy's jaw tightened. It became even tighter when, believing that he should have been given half of the $54,000 prize money, he received nothing. Doc, the youngest man in history to receive this honor, put the entire amount back into the movement, not only rejecting Abernathy's plea but Coretta's as well. She had wanted to use the funds to set up a $5,000 college fund for each of their four children.

It was during the Nobel Prize acceptance speech that Doc expressed his "audacious faith in the future of mankind." He went on, "I refuse to accept the idea that man is mere flotsam and jetsam in the river of life which surrounds him. I refuse to accept the view that mankind is so tragically bound to the starless midnight of racism and war that the bright daybreak of peace and brotherhood can never become a reality.

"I refuse to accept the cynical notion that nation after nation must spiral down a militaristic stairway into the hell of thermonuclear destruction. I believe that unarmed truth and unconditional love will have the final word in reality. That is why right temporarily defeated is stronger than evil triumphant."

The Oslo trip had been planned by Bayard Rustin, the great intellectual strategist who had led Doc to Gandhi's nonviolent philosophy. Bayard is also an unapologetically gay member of the SCLC inner circle. He is now among the most vehement opponents of the Riverside speech. This week at Frogmore there is painful tension between Doc and Bayard. Regarding Rustin, Doc also carries a bit of guilt.

Back in the summer of 1960, Rustin had put together a plan to march on the Democratic National Convention in Los Angeles. This was the convocation that nominated the John Kennedy / Lyndon Johnson ticket to oppose Richard Nixon / Henry Cabot Lodge. The protest was to underscore civil rights issues. But Adam Clayton Powell Jr. of New York, the powerful black congressman and charismatic Harlem minister, opposed the march, viewing it as an unnecessary disruption. When Rustin refused to cancel it, Powell threatened to reveal false information that Doc and Bayard were lovers. Troubled by how such rumors might injure the cause, Doc took his time in making a decision. Meanwhile, convinced of the importance of the demonstration, Rustin took matters into his own hands. He gave up his position as special assistant to King and director of the New York office of SCLC. He expected Doc to reject the resignation. When, in fact, Doc accepted it, Bayard was crushed. A. J. Muste, the brilliant clergyman-activist, wrote that he was "personally ashamed of Martin."

Eventually Rustin went back to work for Doc and planned some of the movement's most spectacular successes. At this moment, though—in May 1967—Bayard's estrangement only adds to Doc's feeling of isolation, even as he walks into the meeting hall, where dozens of staff members are milling about.

Over sweet rolls and coffee there's a feeling of nervous anticipation. Doc is greeted warmly. His subordinates are always excited by his presence, and it's not too often that they see him in an open-collared short-sleeve shirt.

Before things get started, Frieda Mitchell, a teacher who will eventually become the first black school board member in Beaufort County, South Carolina, approaches Doc. She realizes that this may not be the right time or place, but she has wanted to ask him a question for years. She's thinking of all the ugly and humiliating oppression that she has faced as a black woman living in the South.

"How can you tell me to love people who treat me as if I were not human?" she asks Doc.

Doc sees the sincerity in Frieda's eyes. He carefully considers her question. "We are created in God's image," he says. "So you love the image of God in that person."

As the meeting kicks off and his allies confront him about his vision of what SCLC must do this coming summer, Doc tries to remember the words he has just spoken to Frieda. It isn't easy.

The squabbles are endless. The finance committee is complaining about a pile of unpaid phone bills accumulated by Jesse Jackson in Chicago. Staff members from Grenada, Mississippi, lament over the diminishing dedication to nonviolence. How can they stop the militants from winning the minds of the young?

Another segment of the staff argues vociferously that the movement must focus on a Poor People's Campaign in northern cities like Chicago and Cleveland.

Still another segment of impassioned activists maintains that core concentration must remain in the South, where discrimination continues to be the most blatant.

But while they disagree on so much, nearly every member of the staff is certain that, no matter the geographic area, the negative fallout from Riverside has been disastrous. People jump up to argue against the linkage between the civil rights and antiwar movements.

These are bright people, many of whom Doc has recruited himself. These are earnest and hardworking people not afraid to speak their mind. Doc has long supported a symposium where ideas flow freely. He's a firm believer in healthy debate. But the atmosphere at Frogmore goes beyond that. The feeling is personal. Doc's leadership is being questioned. His focus is under attack.

Doc fights back the only way he knows how. He paints the big picture. He says, "We have been in a reform movement...[but] after Selma and the voting rights bill, we moved into a new era, which must be an era of revolution. We must see the great distinction between a reform movement and a revolutionary movement."

Against the charge that he is confusing matters and weakening his cause by joining issues that should be treated separately, he argues, "We must see now that the evils of racism, economic exploitation and militarism are all tied together, [and] you can't really get rid of one without getting rid of the others."

Here it is again—his thesis in a nutshell. Racism, poverty, and militarism. The three-legged monster he sees destroying the American dream. The three-legged monster he sees destroying the American soul. It grieves him that his supporters don't see it that way. He needs them to back him up. He yearns for allies. But ultimately, even if it means the corrosion of his authority within the organization he founded, he cannot yield on core principles.

"When I took up the cross," he tells the group, "I recognized its meaning.... The cross is something that you bear and ultimately that you die on. The cross may mean the death of your popularity.... It may mean the death of a foundation grant. It may cut your budget down a little, but take up your cross and just bear it. And that is the way I have decided to go."

Doc's cross is his unyielding stand against the war.

When he reads the papers and political journals, all evidence points to the fact that the pro-war LBJ administration is more adamant than ever. When he reads about the casualties, his heart sinks: 1,380 Americans will die in Vietnam in May alone, making it the bloodiest month yet. Since the start of the conflict, 13,368 American lives have been lost. God only knows the number of fallen Vietnamese. Estimates put it at hundreds of thousands. And it's only getting worse.

There is no way for Doc to know that there is growing division among LBJ's senior advisers. Secretary of Defense Robert McNamara, one of the war's chief architects, is expressing grave doubts about the efficacy of the bombing. He's also questioning the validity of the domino theory — that if we don't stop communism in North Vietnam, all of

Indochina will fall. But McNamara's relatively dovish views are falling on deaf ears. The president is leaning on hardcore hawks like General William Westmoreland, commander of the U.S. forces in Vietnam, who believes that the policy of attrition is working and that more force will eventually cripple the Vietcong. Decades later, historian Taylor Branch will write that Johnson "backed into Vietnam with Cold War inertia bottomed on his naked political fear of being called a coward."

Most of the war's critics within LBJ's administration, like McNamara, will retreat in the name of loyalty to their president. The White House will grow more arrogant in its insistence that this war is essential in protecting American interests. Opponents like Doc will grow bolder in their insistence that the war is morally corrupt and unnecessary.

In America, all the gaps are widening.

The same is true in Doc's own life, where there is a growing gap between him and his family. The separation between Doc, a man in continual motion, and his wife and children takes a terrible toll, contributing to his feelings of heavy guilt.

Then there is the gap between him and his former supporters in the Negro mainstream establishment. This week's meeting has shown his staff in open revolt. And his loyal Jewish backers—namely attorney Stanley Levison and Rabbi Abraham Joshua Heschel—are highly critical of his antiwar stance.

The turbulent Frogmore conference comes to an end. There has been no time for softball games but plenty for a prolonged series of heated disputations. Rather than feeling refreshed by the retreat, Doc is exhausted. As he prepares to leave the island, he reads a piece in *Newsweek* that has him reflecting on Levison and Heschel, and then one that explains how President Nasser of Egypt has denied Israel the use of the Straits of Tiran, a vital shipping lane from the Red Sea. Israel is threatened.

On the drive back down Highway 21 to the Savannah airport, Doc considers what this threat means. Inevitably — and understandably — Jewish interest will turn from the three-prong evils that never leave Doc's mind: racism, poverty, and militarism. Jewish interest will focus on the survival of the Jewish nation. Before the month is over, Levison himself will complain that the antiwar effort is "suffering badly because half the peace movement is Jewish, and the Jews have all become hawks."

The clouds of war are darkening — war in Southeast Asia, and now the ominous prospect of war in the Middle East.

War weighs on Doc's mind as he returns home only long enough to kiss Coretta and the kids, pack a bag, and catch a plane from Atlanta to New York, where he will board still another plane and make still another trip, this one across the Atlantic to an international conference in Geneva, where the topic will be the world's obsession with war.

It is in neutral Switzerland that Doc will denounce the Vietnam War as "costly, bloody and futile."

"If we assume that life is worth living and that man has a right to survive," he says before the august body of assorted diplomats and scholars, "we must find an alternative to war. In a day when vehicles hurtle through outer space and guided ballistic missiles carve highways of death through the stratosphere and napalm flames destroy God's green earth and his children, no nation can claim victory in war."

It is at this same conference that he sees the delegates' attention switch from Hanoi and Saigon to Cairo and Tel Aviv.

The conference is quick. Doc is back on a plane heading home. He reads, he drinks, he smokes, he sleeps, he dreams. He awakes in the middle of the night, not quite realizing where he is. The newspaper on his lap says it is the start of June. An attack on Israel is imminent. More than a hundred thousand Egyptian troops are amassed in the Sinai desert along with nearly a thousand tanks. Seventy-five thousand Syrian troops stand ready at that country's border with Israel. Additionally, Jordan has fifty-five thousand troops and three hundred tanks.

Doc knows it's only a matter of days.

He rustles through his attaché case and finds an advance copy of his new book, due out later this very month, *Where Do We Go from Here: Chaos or Community?*

He ponders the question.

*Chapter Six*

———————

# WHERE DO WE GO FROM HERE?

Doc's close associates love to analyze his motives, methods, and psychology. This is only natural. Charismatic characters are always subjects of speculation. We want to know what makes them tick. Some say that Doc's feverish drive is fueled by the pure passion of his sociopolitical convictions. Others say that his restlessness is rooted in some deep dissatisfaction with a conventional church-and-home life that cannot pacify his adventuresome spirit. Some view him as a modern version of the itinerant country preacher, traveling from one community to another to spread the Word.

Doc has heard all these theories, and while they hold some interest for him — he is, after all, no stranger to introspection — he ultimately dismisses the conjecture. He may be exhausted, he may be despondent, he is surely battle weary, but that's not important: all that matters is that he has a plane to catch, a rally to attend, a war to stop.

The Six-Day War shocks the world. The armies and air power surrounding Israel are decimated with deadly precision. It is a historic victory for the Jewish state and a crushing blow for Egypt, Jordan, Syria, and Iraq. It also changes the dynamic of the Negro-Jewish coalition in America that has long fought for civil rights and, more recently, protested the war in Vietnam.

Doc is a staunch supporter of Israel. A week before the war, he was one of eight church leaders who signed a letter to the *New York Times* urging the Johnson administration to back Israel. Among his closest colleagues, though, he expresses concern that the very nature of the sweeping victory — and the fact that Israel has occupied the Sinai, the Golan Heights, and the West Bank of the Jordan River — could injure the soul of the Jewish state. The captured land gives Israel a defensive buffer against its sworn enemies. But now some six hundred thousand Arabs will be living in the West Bank under Israeli control. "Israel," Doc tells his confidantes, "faces the danger of being smug and unyielding."

Once seen as the underdog fighting for its very survival, Israel is suddenly transformed into a military power of unprecedented effectiveness. The nation is now an occupying power. And while the lightning victory has emboldened the spirits of Jews worldwide and, in the aftermath of Hitler's Holocaust, given credence to the cry "Never again!," Doc worries about an impact on the antiwar movement in America. As he says to Stanley Levison, "It has given Johnson the little respite he wanted from Vietnam."

Two conflicting movements are on the rise: a significant segment of American Jews is becoming increasingly obsessed with Israel while black nationalism is finding favor among black youth. Doc stands outside both of these movements. His drive to underscore the evils of poverty, racism, and militarism does not fit into a paradigm of nationalism, Jewish or black.

Doc feels the tension building and races up to New York on June 12 for a secret meeting at Union Theological Seminary with, among others, activist priest Daniel Berrigan and Rabbi Abraham Joshua Heschel. The rabbi, recently returned from Jerusalem, is ecstatic over the Israeli victory. "It is as if," he says, "the prophets had risen from their graves."

Doc worries about what reveling in military victory will do to the spirit of nonviolence. His own spirit is further assaulted when on this same day the Supreme Court, in a five to four decision, grants the state of Alabama the right to reimprison him for his refusal to follow a 1963 injunction that prohibited him from protesting in Birmingham. It doesn't matter that an editorial in the *New York Times* calls the decision "profoundly embarrassing to the good name of the United States" or that Chief Justice Earl Warren has vigorously dissented. Doc is going back to jail.

"Even the Supreme Court has turned against us," he tells his friends.

* * *

The next day Lyndon Johnson nominates Thurgood Marshall to the Supreme Court. Once confirmed, he will be America's first Negro high court justice. As the man who successfully argued the 1953 *Brown v. Board of Education* case outlawing public school segregation, Marshall is a highly respected attorney — although he is no fan of Martin Luther King Jr.

Unlike Doc, Marshall backs Johnson on Vietnam. He also opposes Doc's protest marches and civil disobedience, calling him a "boy on a man's errand." Later he will reluctantly acknowledge King's role as a leader, saying, "As an organizer he wasn't worth shit.... He was a great speaker... but as for getting the work done, he was not too good at that.... All he did was to dump all his legal work on us [the NAACP], including the bills. And that was all right with him, so long as he didn't have to pay the bills."

No love is lost between Doc and Thurgood, and no time is wasted during Doc's appearance on ABC's Sunday morning news program *Issues and Answers,* where he is asked about the infighting among Negro leaders. As usual, Doc rises to the occasion. He takes the high road.

"No movement worth its salt is devoid of philosophical debate," he tells the national audience, "and there are moments in any social revolution where you have peaks of united activity and you have other moments of debate and even dissension."

A reporter quotes *Where Do We Go from Here* to question the soundness of Doc's approach as laid out in his new text. Doc has written, "We [the Negro community] must develop, from strength, a situation in which the government finds it wise and prudent to collaborate with us."

"How can you speak out against the administration's policies in Vietnam," asks a journalist, "and achieve this end? Aren't you in effect defeating the purpose?"

Doc replies, "We have never achieved anything, we haven't made a single gain without the confrontation of power with power."

When asked to comment on the Middle East, he asserts, "All people of good will must respect the territorial integrity of Israel.... We must see what Israel has done for the world. It is a marvelous demonstration of what people together in unity and with rugged determination can do in transforming almost a desert land into an oasis. But the other side is that peace in the Middle East means something else.... The Arab world is part of that third world of poverty and illiteracy and disease and it is time now to have a Marshall Plan for the Middle East.... We must see that there is a grave refugee problem that the Arabs have."

Before the interview is over, Doc's support of Muhammad Ali is challenged once again. Given that Ali is a man who makes his living fighting in a ring, isn't it inconsistent for him to refuse to fight for his country?

"I don't find it inconsistent at all," says Doc. "I find it

a very great act of courage." He adds that he hopes Ali's position "will cause many young people to take a greater stand against the draft and to refuse to fight in the war in Vietnam."

*Where Do We Go from Here: Chaos or Community?* is published with little fanfare. The road to publication has been rocky. When Doc first showed the text to Stanley Levison, his friend was alarmed by the absence of fresh material. He pointed out that Doc was actually plagiarizing from his previous book, *Why We Can't Wait*. Doc owned up to his mistake, writing to his editor, "I made a definite literary mistake.... I lifted a great deal of what I had said in the last chapter of *Why We Can't Wait* because I felt it was so relevant at this point."

Doc did write a new chapter analyzing Black Power that the publisher felt was strong enough to garner interest. Yet Joan Daves, Doc's literary agent, encounters stiff resistance in her attempt to sell an excerpt of the book. Doc's politics are considered too well-known and obvious. The media wants something new and strong, not a rehash of previous positions.

The reviews are lukewarm to outright hostile.

Eliot Fremont-Smith, in the *New York Times,* mentions Doc's advocacy of "legal political Black Power" and his call for a "return to nonviolence, an alignment of Negroes and poor whites to force the massive Federal poverty-civil rights program once advocated by the President."

In *Commonweal* magazine, though, David Steinberg claims that "King's book seems to be groping for something which it never finds." He sees Doc in a state of "great confusion and doubt."

Writing in the *New York Review of Books,* one of the most prestigious intellectual journals in the country, Andrew Kopkind is caustic: "He [King] has simply, and disastrously, arrived at the wrong conclusions about the world.... Whites have ceased to believe him, or really to care; the blacks hardly listen." Viewing Doc as the standard-bearer of liberalism, Kopkind writes that issues surrounding the Vietnam War and black militancy "have contrived this summer to murder liberalism...and there are few mourners."

Realizing the devastating effect of these barbed reviews, Stanley Levison sends a more positive notice from the *Washington Post,* along with a letter to Doc in which he writes, "Many of the reviewers seem to be so pessimistic they are shaken up because you are not in black despair. I believe they are reflecting the unhappy defeatist mood of intellectual America at the moment. The fact that the book insists on not burying the positive indicates how much this lesson needed to be expressed."

In the *Post,* Martin Duberman sees the book as Doc's attempt "to summarize the recent conflicts within the civil rights movement, to consider the larger context, both national and international, which helps to account for these conflicts, and finally, to suggest possible lines for action." He points to Doc's practical programs versus Stokely Carmichael's reliance on slogans without substance. "Yet when

King himself comes to spelling out a program for pooling black resources, economic and political, its stock generalities prove vulnerably close to Carmichael's sloganeering." In the end, the review concludes on a pessimistic note: "King's position seems to me impeccable in theory, but it suffers, as he himself must realize, from the lack of available allies for the coalition he advocates."

The lack of allies.

In a year of best sellers like William Manchester's tome on Kennedy — *The Death of a President* — Doc's book sells poorly and soon vanishes from the shelves.

Doc is out of style and out of step. Even the language of the day outdates him: he is the ultimate Negro at a time when Negroes are seeing themselves as blacks. The hope that his new text might reassert his relevance — by quieting his critics and winning back those increasingly disillusioned with his nonviolent strategy — has been dashed. On a professional level, there can be no doubt: Doc has the blues.

On a personal level, Doc's blues deepen when, on a Saturday night in the third week of June, he gets a frantic call from brother A. D. in Louisville.

In light of the Supreme Court decision that came down earlier in the month, A. D. is ranting about how he, along with Doc and others, will have to go back to jail. But it's more than a political rant that Doc is hearing from his brother. A. D. has fallen into a drunken stupor. He has suffered with debilitating depression before, but this time he speaks of taking his own life.

The words chill Doc's heart and take him back to a

dark childhood day. It was 1941. Martin was twelve years old; A. D. was eleven. It was a morning when Martin was keen on seeing a local parade. He loved the brassy sounds of marching bands and the sight of the high-stepping majorettes. He had chores to do at home and his mother and father nixed the idea, but Martin had a stubborn streak and defied his parents. He ran off to watch the parade.

A few hours later, he returned home to a tragic scene. His maternal grandmother, whom he adored, had suffered a fatal heart attack. Sliding down a banister, A. D. had unwittingly crashed into her and knocked her to the floor. Martin blamed himself. If he hadn't run off to the parade, he would have been around to supervise his brother — and his grandmother would still be alive. Later he would be told that her encounter with A. D. did not cause the heart attack. But that was after Martin was so despondent that, in what he later called a suicide attempt, he jumped from the second story of the family home. He was merely bruised, but the bruises to his psyche were severe and long lasting. For days he wouldn't leave his bedroom.

Serious melancholia plagued Doc as a child and as an adult. The same was true for brother A. D.

Now, alarmed by A. D.'s threats to take his own life, Doc gets on the phone and rounds up a group of his Louisville friends to minister to his brother. His friends are able — at least for the time being — to bring his brother around.

The blues are on Doc's mind the next day, a Sunday morning, as he ascends to the pulpit to preach at Ebenezer in Atlanta. Not just his blues and his brother's blues but America's blues. Hawk versus dove, young versus old, black versus white, black versus Negro—it feels as though his country, like his brother, is on the verge of a nervous collapse. These are dark, dark days.

In contrast to darkness, Doc preaches about light. Darkness is brought on by ingratitude, the subject of his sermon. The dangers of ingratitude are many, and the antidote, of course, is gratitude. Gratitude, Doc argues, is what protects us from arrogance. Gratitude is our link to sanity. He talks about a rich Negro who boasts in public of his exalted position without giving gratitude to the man and woman who brought him into the world. Without gratitude, ego runs amok. Without gratitude, there is no humility. Doc points out that "we wouldn't have a civil rights bill today if some three thousand children hadn't packed up the jails in Birmingham, Alabama." Gratitude grounds us in God. "Ingratitude," he preaches, "is a sin because it causes one to fail to realize his dependence on God." He sees God as the creative power of the universe.

Doc's preaching reaches beyond the realm of practical politics or moral behavior. He lifts the congregation—he lifts himself—with talk of dreams and blessed sleep.

"You dream," he says, "and you dream about things and you see things and you are away from everything. But then early in the morning you wake up. That's a miracle to me. And this morning I want to thank God for sleep."

"Sure we got the blues," blues singer John Lee Hooker

once said. "But singing the blues is how we lose the blues. When we singing, we free."

In the sanctity of the pulpit, Doc loses his blues — if only for the moment. His words relieve the burdens weighing on his heart. His blues sermons are exercises of praise and worship that allow him to transcend the mundane and rise above the muck and mire of a nasty world marred in endless disputation. His blues sermons allow him to soar. They strengthen his resolve and fortify his troubled soul.

This is Sunday, the Lord's day.

But here comes Monday. For good reason they call it stormy Monday, and Tuesday's just as bad. Doc is back in the world of endless disputations, an all-too-real world that grows nastier by the day.

## Chapter Seven

# CITIES AFLAME

In his conservative coat and tie, Doc is standing in the wings. At a time when other black leaders are sporting outfits that reflect the mood of the day — dashikis, leather jackets, dark glasses, and berets — Doc is unchanging. His black suits symbolize what he calls "coffin ready."

Today he is ready to drum up interest in his new book. A large studio audience awaits his appearance on live national television. Former big band singer and congenial talk show host Merv Griffin introduces him as "one of the great voices in America." Doc steps out to a standing ovation. Griffin greets him warmly, as does Merv's first guest, Harry Belafonte.

Having heard that, behind his serious demeanor, Doc is a fun-loving man known for his jocular behavior, Merv starts off on a light note.

"You've discovered [New York is] a fun city?" he asks Doc.

"Well, I haven't quite discovered that side of New York. Being a Baptist clergyman, they keep me involved in other areas."

So much for the humor.

Merv quickly moves to the grave matters of the day. It is July and there is concern that the heat of summer mixed with the scalding discontent in America's great urban centers will result in riots. In the past, protestors like Doc have been blamed for provoking civil unrest.

"You can't blame nonviolent demonstrators who are demonstrating for their constitutional rights when violence erupts," Doc tells Merv. "This would be like blaming the robbed man for the evil act of robbery because his possession of wealth, money, precipitates the act. Society must always condemn the robber and protect the robbed....

"This is like looking at a physician, who, through his skills, through his medical ingenuity, discovers cancer in a patient, and blaming the doctor for causing the cancer. It's usually the other way around. We praise the physician for using his ingenuity to bring out into the open something that needed to be discovered and something that can be cured if it is caught early enough. And this is exactly what we have done. We can't be blamed for the violence that emerges. We've merely brought it out in the open. We've brought the evil conditions, the cancerous disease of racism, out in the open. And far from being the cause of it, we are merely the catalytic agents bringing it out for everybody to see so that society can cure it."

As the interview continues, Doc's new book is barely mentioned. He realizes that he has done a poor job of promoting his book. He also wonders if he has done an equally poor job of promoting his views.

Doc's views have never been an easy sell. Seven years ago, when he was the rising star of the civil rights movement, his views did not persuade J. H. Jackson, president of the National Baptist Convention, U.S.A. Inc., and perhaps the most powerful black preacher in America. Despite the success of the Montgomery Bus Boycott, Jackson sternly rejected Doc's strategy of civil disobedience. Jackson's intransigence convinced Doc that the man had to be replaced. With help from other like-minded minister-activists, Doc supported the candidacy of Reverend Dr. Gardner C. Taylor in hopes that he would replace Jackson.

At the National Baptist Convention's annual meeting in Philadelphia in 1960, Taylor won the election. A year later, though, when the group reconvened in Kansas City, Jackson stepped to the podium and flat out refused to give up his presidency. The protest against him took a violent turn. There was pandemonium on the platform. One supporter of Jackson's fell to the floor, struck his head, and died of a concussion. And Jackson blamed the death on Martin Luther King Jr. Doc, who had not been in the hall when the fight erupted, fired back, "Such an unwarranted, untrue, and unethical statement is libelous to the core and can do irreparable harm to the freedom movement in which I am involved." As a result, Doc left the National Baptist Convention and helped form the Progressive National Baptist Convention.

Doc's progressive politics have always troubled large segments of the black church. J. H. Jackson is not alone in questioning Doc's tactics. As a representative of the black bourgeoisie, Jackson cannot understand how a respectable minister like Doc can defiantly march in the streets and openly break the law. Like Thurgood Marshall, Jackson feels threatened by tactics that he considers beneath Doc's educational and social stature. After all, Doc holds a bachelor's degree from Morehouse College with a major in sociology; a bachelor's of divinity from Crozer Theological Seminary; a PhD in the philosophy of systematic theology from Boston University; and honorary degrees from, among others, Howard University, Chicago Theological Seminary, Bard College, Wesleyan College, Yale University, and Oberlin College.

When Doc's dad helped arrange his first pastorate — at the Dexter Avenue Baptist Church in Montgomery, Alabama — even he, Daddy King, did not initially approve of his son's street protests. Ever since then, Doc's attempt to win over the heart and soul of the middle-class black church has been a long and often unsuccessful effort.

Toward the end of the Merv Griffin interview, Doc wonders whether he has won over the heart and soul of this largely white audience. When he is asked about what the civil rights movement has ultimately done for blacks, Doc doesn't point to legislation as the greatest accomplishment; he points to positive self-identity. He says that the movement "has given the Negro a new sense of dignity. A new sense of somebodyness. And this is maybe the greatest victory that we have won.... The Negro has a sense of pride now that he has desperately needed all along. And he is able to stand up and feel that he is a man.... The Negro has straightened his back up...and you can't ride a man's back unless it's bent."

At the end of the interview, Doc stands up. His own back is straight. In public appearances such as these, he fortifies his position. Although his national stature is sinking fast, amiable show business figures like Merv Griffin, encouraged by faithful friends like Harry Belafonte, are still willing to give Doc his say.

Maybe his new book will catch on after all. Maybe the month of July will be a time when the world will recognize the relevance and current value of Martin Luther King's undying commitment to the creed of nonviolence. Doc knows that militant slogans sound sexy, but surely they repel the great mass of Negroes seeking justice rather than the fleeting satisfaction of mindless violence. For a moment, Doc is optimistic.


His optimism dies a sudden and awful death on July 14. Sitting at home at 234 Sunset Avenue in Vine City, a historic black neighborhood in Atlanta, Doc's heart sinks as he watches the televised news reports on Newark. New Jersey's most populous city is imploding. It is a city that, due to white flight to the suburbs, is among the first in America to have a Negro majority. Abject poverty has long plagued that majority. Rampant unemployment, racial profiling, police brutality, and stunted educational opportunities have been wracking Newark for years. Like so many urban ghettoes, the city has been a smoldering tinderbox. It has the nation's highest percentage of substandard housing and the second highest percentage of crime and infant mortality. Doc can't be surprised by the outbreak of violence. He realizes that its cause is far more than a rumor that the police have murdered a black cabdriver who was taken into custody for a minor traffic infraction. Yet even though many have predicted that bloody riots would erupt during this incredibly tense summer, Doc has been hoping against hope that such conflagrations might be avoided. He has been praying for peace.

Just as the Six-Day War in June undercut the notion of peace in the Middle East, this four-day riot in July is undercutting the notion of peace in America's chocolate cities. In Newark the destruction does not discriminate. Whether public or private, property is torched. Roving bands of rioters go on all-night looting binges. Black owners attempting to avert disaster by writing "Soul bro" on the windows of their businesses are largely ignored. Rage overpowers reason. As if in answer to Doc's current book—*Where Do We Go from Here: Chaos or Community?*—chaos rules.

On the third day, National Guardsmen and state troopers start firing. By the time the riot is quelled, there are nearly fifteen hundred arrests, more than seven hundred injuries, and twenty-six deaths. When Doc reads that among those killed is Edward Moss, a ten-year-old boy, the same age of his own son Martin III, his eyes are wet with tears.

To those who will listen, Doc condemns the riots while pointing to the corrosive conditions that created them. The press, though, is far more interested in headlining the reactions of the militants.

On July 18, a day after Newark is finally quiet, the *New York Times* reports that in nearby Jersey City, "H. Rap Brown, special director of the Student Nonviolent Coordinating Committee, exhorted about 100 Negroes tonight to 'wage guerrilla war on the honkie white man'.... Mr. Brown and other militant Black Power leaders had sought to organize a big rally to obtain the release of 13 Negro youths arrested Monday night on charges of looting.... Mr. Brown told an interviewer, 'If they don't let them out, we're going to burn this courthouse down.'"

Deeply disturbed that leaders of a "nonviolent" group are openly advocating violence, Doc considers speaking out. He wants to protest what he sees as a perverted turn on the part of the protestors. But time has run out. In the past, Doc had always moved ahead of the curve; he had always marched at the head of the parade. But in this vicious summer of discontent, there is no orderly march, no disciplined parade. This is the summer of mayhem and misery.

Barely a week after Newark, Detroit erupts in what will be an even deadlier riot. This time President Johnson responds quickly. Minutes after receiving a request from Michigan governor George Romney, LBJ orders Secretary of Defense McNamara to airlift five thousand federal troops to Detroit. Depending on your point of view, American troops are either defending or attacking American citizens.

From Cuba, where he has traveled in defiance of the State Department, Stokely Carmichael praises Castro for standing up to the United States and declares, "We must recognize that Detroit and New York are also Vietnam."

In Cambridge, Maryland, where he is wounded by shotgun fire, H. Rap Brown characterizes what is happening in Detroit: "This ain't no riot, brother. This is a rebellion, and we got 400 years of reason to tear this town apart."

LBJ addresses the nation and says, "We will not tolerate lawlessness. We will not endure violence. It matters not by whom it is done or under what slogan or banner. It will not be tolerated. This nation will do whatever it is necessary to do to suppress and to punish those who engage in it."

Here's the president, justifying his policy of bloody escalation in Vietnam, attempting to stop the bloodshed at home.

The next day Doc feels compelled to respond. As he sits at home in front of the television watching the tanks roll through the streets of Detroit, he sends the president a telegram that he later reads at a press conference at Ebenezer Baptist Church. He neither questions the president's decision to send troops to Detroit nor attacks the militants' view of the riot as a revolutionary act. Instead he uses the moment to point out the urgent need for immediate legislation to correct the conditions that caused the violence. He excoriates Congress for "moral degradation."

"Though the aimless violence and destruction may be contained through military means, only drastic changes in the life of the poor will provide the kind of order and stability you desire," he tells LBJ. "There is no question that the violence and destruction of property must be halted, but Congress has consistently refused to vote a halt [to] the destruction of the lives of Negroes in the ghetto."

In this same telegram, Doc does more than lament the recent rejection of rent supplement legislation and even "a simple bill to protect our cities against rats. The suicidal and irrational acts which plague our streets daily are being sowed and watered by the irrational, irrelevant and equally suicidal debate and delay in Congress." He lays out a plan to "end unemployment totally and immediately.... If our government cannot create jobs, it cannot govern. It cannot have white affluence amid black poverty and have racial harmony.

"The turmoil of the ghetto is the externalization of the Negro's inner torment and rage."

During the press conference, when asked if he'll go to Detroit to help stop the ongoing riots, Doc demurs. Such a trip would be futile. "I feel that my job," he says, "is to work in communities to build the programs and to try to bring about the response from administrations that will prevent riots."

He reminds the reporters that he has lived in the slums of Chicago and Cleveland and plans to return to those cities this summer to continue the work to heal the terrible wounds bleeding the life out of the nation's teeming ghettoes. As usual, Doc puts on a brave face. He says what he believes. Violence only breeds more violence. Practical measures, advocated through persistent and peaceful protests, must be realized to relieve the suffering of the downtrodden trapped in the hopeless cycle of poverty and despair.

But his public statements do not relieve his own despair. He suffers for his people, the people of Newark and the people of Detroit, the people across the country who will live through more than 125 riots before summer is over. He feels helpless.

He remembers this same awful feeling of helplessness when, two years ago, he went to Los Angeles in the wake of Watts. Ironically, the riots in Los Angeles broke out six days after the passage of the Voting Rights Act, a major achievement of the movement. He arrived in the burned-out ghetto while the fires were still simmering. The devastation was heartbreaking.

Seeing two young looters walking down the street, Doc got out of his car and approached them. At first they didn't recognize him. He asked them what motivated them to do what they had done.

"We won," said one of the men. "Don't you understand— *we won!* We showed these white people!"

"What did you win?" asked Doc. "What do you have to show for it? What is the point of all this?"

Recognizing Doc and realizing just who was addressing him, the second young man took a moment to think about the questions.

"At least we made them pay attention."

Doc had no answer. All he could think of was how all people require attention. All people require respect. All people require acknowledgment. All people require love.

*But what a desperately sad and self-destructive way to gain it!*

Later he warned the people of Watts against hating whites, reminding them that "when we marched from Selma to Montgomery, it was a white woman — Viola Liuzzo — who died on that Highway 80," referring to the civil rights protestor murdered by the Ku Klux Klan.

That was Selma. That was Watts. But today is different. Today is Detroit, a city whose people are not clamoring to hear from Martin Luther King Jr., who remains in Atlanta.

Doc may be a dreamer, but he's also a realist. And he can't deny his precipitous loss of influence with the Johnson administration to support the legislation that he favors — the very legislation that he feels may prevent further riots. Never has he been out of favor with so many factions.

The faction that works hardest against him is undoubtedly the FBI, which continues to secretly monitor his every move. Hoover redoubles his pernicious efforts to destroy him. In wiretapping a conversation between Doc and Levison, the director misinterprets Doc's remarks and runs to LBJ, insisting that King is planning to incite riots and take over Chicago's Loop. While Doc bemoans his ineffectiveness as a peacemaker, Hoover maligns him as an instigator, further eroding the president's faith in his former ally's intentions.

For five long, agonizing days, Detroit continues to burn. By the time the troops put down the looters, more than fifteen hundred buildings are torched. Destroyed property is valued at more than $100 million. Most tragically, forty-three people are dead. The riot is called the worst the country has suffered in the past hundred years.

*  *  *

Coretta and Doc's closest aides worry about him. They discover him, usually a model of self-restraint, openly weeping.

On August 2, he's due to fly from Atlanta to Louisville, where he has promised to address the urgent need for voter registration. This time, though, he simply can't get on the plane. Despondency has rendered him inert.

"I know why I missed my flight," he tells Coretta from an airport pay phone. "I really don't want to go. I get tired of going and not having any answers. People feel that non-violence is failing."

"But this is not so," Coretta replies. "You mustn't believe that people are losing faith in you. There are millions of people who have faith in you and believe in you and feel that you are our best hope.... I believe in you, if that means anything."

"Yes," says Doc. "It means a great deal."

Doc finds the wherewithal to wait at the airport for the next flight to Louisville. He's seven hours late to the city, but somehow he makes it to his speech on time. He delivers the address. He fulfills his commitment. And then it's back on the plane, back home to Atlanta, back to reading dire newspaper reports about the fallout from last month's riots.

He ruminates on the flight home. As appalling as the war in Vietnam might be, it is a world away. But these riots—these horrific nightmares in which black people are burning down black neighborhoods—are on American soil.

These are the neighborhoods in which he has toiled for the past twelve years. He knows now that everything he has worked for is in danger of dying. How can he reconcile his sacred belief in nonviolence with this, the most violent summer in the history of his movement? The short-lived period of landmark legislation is gone. An embittered and divided Congress is unwilling to respond to the needs of the poor. Despite massive protests, the foreign war escalates. Despite the call for calm, the domestic situation deteriorates.

Fire is more than a metaphor. Fire is a reality on the streets of black America. Burning cities, burning hopes, burning bridges to reason and righteousness.

The plane lands with a thud on the Atlanta runway, snapping Doc back into the moment. A waiting car speeds him home. He is happy to be in his own house. He embraces Coretta and looks in on his precious children, who have already gone to sleep. He envies their easy sleep. He needs sleep himself. But sleep does not come. He struggles through the night, and at daybreak he prays for strength.

## Chapter Eight

# RESPECT

In one form or another, strength returns. Doc fights through exhaustion and frustration. He does not give in to what he calls "the luxury of despair." His resilient character moves even those who oppose him within his own movement. In the face of his fiercest assailants, he is charitable to a fault. He listens carefully. He patiently considers their points of view. Facing an adversary, he seeks to bring to each conversation a sense of understanding. There are times when he stumbles, but his aim never changes: every day he works to deepen his compassion.

Some of his closest observers, like Vincent Harding, his Atlanta neighbor who drafted the Riverside speech, are convinced that they are watching a man being born again. In the Book of John, when Jesus tells Nicodemus that "except a man be born again, he cannot see the kingdom of God," Nicodemus is perplexed. How can a man reenter his mother's womb to experience a second birth? Jesus's answer is that this rebirth is "of water and of the Spirit."

Harding is certain that Doc is being rebaptized in the spiritual realm of a greater God consciousness. Doc's former concerns about the racist policies restricting the civil and voting rights of black folks have largely been addressed. But now it is becoming increasingly evident that his wider concerns—his distress over the crippling effects of poverty, racism, and militarism—have radically broadened his work and witness.

While Doc is experiencing a spiritual rebirth, he is calling for a rebirth of America itself. The nation's initial birth—with its genocidal treatment of Native Americans and inhumane enslavement of African Americans—must be reexamined. In his recent book, he wrote, "Ever since the birth of our nation, white America has had a schizophrenic personality on the question of race. She has been torn between selves—a self in which she proudly professed the great principles of democracy and a self in which she sadly practiced the antithesis of democracy.... What is the source of this perennial indecision and vacillation? It lies in the 'congenital deformity' of racism that has crippled the nation from its inception."

At Riverside, Doc said, "A true revolution of values will soon cause us to question the fairness and justice of many of our past and present policies. On the one hand we are called to play the Good Samaritan on life's roadside, but that will be only an initial act. One day we must come to see that the whole Jericho Road must be transformed so that men and women will not be constantly beaten and robbed as they make their journey on life's highway. True compassion is more than flinging a coin to a beggar. It comes to see that an edifice which produces beggars needs restructuring."

Doc understands that the angry reaction to his call for this rebirth concerns, in part, money. His victories for integration and equality did not carry a price tag; they represented no monetary cost to America. But now Doc is demanding that we reexamine our economic priorities. He insists that budgets are moral documents. It is transparently immoral to pay the outrageous price of a reckless military adventure while cutting out the very heart of our domestic social programs. In no uncertain terms, he brings home the point: bombs being dropped in Vietnam are landing in the ghettoes of America.

Such statements threaten both white and black America.

White America has told Doc: We have created a space for you. We have allowed you to be the leader of your people for your cause. We have become comfortable seeing you in this space. This space has resulted in your receiving a Nobel Peace Prize. But that leadership and prize do not allow you to address issues outside your space.

And when Doc addresses those issues head-on, other mainstream black leaders react in fear. One after another, major Negro figures abandon Doc. For centrists like Carl Rowan, Doc is too far to the left. For leftists like H. Rap Brown, Doc is too much a centrist. Among those who continue to denounce him publicly and privately are Roy Wilkins and Whitney Young, who lead the NAACP and the Urban League, respectively; clergyman and congressman Adam Clayton Powell Jr.; and legal giant Thurgood Marshall. Some are essentially surrogates for the White House, men unwilling to side with anyone who dares to defy a president.

But it isn't all bad. In the summer of 1967, Aretha Franklin's "Respect," a number-one hit on both the rhythm-and-blues and pop charts, does nothing but help the movement. With its irresistible rhythms and insistent upbeat cry, the song is an anthem for not only the right of a woman to be respected by her man but the right of a people to be respected by a nation.

In mid-August, as Doc walks into the ballroom of an Atlanta hotel to address a convention of black radio deejays, "Respect" is blasting over the loudspeakers. In the form of a long and rousing standing ovation, respect is exactly what the deejays afford Doc. They are especially gratified that he has agreed to deliver the keynote speech.

Like his good friend Reverend C. L. Franklin, Aretha's illustrious father and head of Detroit's New Bethel Baptist Church, Doc has decried the old myth embraced by many in the black community that sacred and secular music are incompatible, that you're either singing the gospel's good news or the devil's soul-crushing blues. Doc has celebrated the genius of worldly rhythm and blues before. Today, at this convocation, he reminisces about his love of soul music. He praises the work of legendary deejays like Pervis "The Blues Man" Spann in Chicago, Magnificent Montague in Los Angeles, and Georgie Woods in Philadelphia. He acknowledges how deejay "Tall Paul" White helped mobilize the massive nonviolent demonstrations in Birmingham back in '63. He recognizes the role that black popular music — manifest in stirring songs like "Respect" — has played in freeing the hearts and minds of a people searching for a strong self-identity.

"You introduced youth to that music and created the language of soul," he says, "and promoted the dance which now sweeps across race, class, and nation. It is quite amazing to me to hear the youthful rhythms which I found time to enjoy as a youth here in Atlanta years ago coming back across the Atlantic with an English accent."

He speaks about the American nation that has "produced machines that think and instruments that peer into the unfathomable ranges of interstellar space" and yet faces the challenge of "transforming a neighborhood into a brotherhood."

He speaks about the deep roots of racism — "the black man's burden and the white man's shame" — and how history has conspired to reinforce that racism. The problem of racial injustice, he argues, cannot be solved without persistent nonviolent pressure. He contrasts that to the philosophy of Booker T. Washington, who "believed that the problem could be solved through pressure-less persuasion." But for Doc, Washington "misread history.... He started saying everything that the white people wanted to hear. He was honored for it. He was called a responsible leader. I always get a little worried when I'm referred to as a responsible leader because...they are really telling you that you are a leader who will not tell the truth on behalf of your people....Booker T. Washington went on with the notion of pressure-less persuasion and the reactionary forces of the white South used that only to plunge deeper into the oppression of the Negro. He told us to let our buckets down where we were, and the problem was that there wasn't much water in the well.

"Somewhere we must come to see that we must rise up and stand on our own two feet and say to our white brothers that we are determined to be men. That is what the movement is saying. We are somebody. We are determined to gain our freedom. And we are going to start with ourselves by freeing our own psyche, our own souls."

After the speech, Aretha's "Respect" is revived. The song plays another three or four times before the evening is over.

After a late-night flight to New York, Doc is shown little respect by the reporters grilling him on NBC's *Meet the Press*. One, in fact, is looking to nail him for the riots.

"Some of your strongest critics have charged that you yourself are responsible for part of the urban violence that afflicts us recently in the riots, in that by advocating civil disobedience the logical and inevitable effect of that is civil disorder, that people who have no respect for law and authority then take things into their own hands. How do you answer such charges?"

Doc is quick to respond, calling the accusation "absurd." "I have never advocated anarchy," he says. "I have never advocated arson, I have never advocated sniping or looting. I have only said, and I still believe this, that if one finds a law unjust, then he has a moral responsibility to take a stand against that law, even if it means breaking that law."

He goes on to point out that "less than 1 percent of the Negroes of our country have engaged in riots. More than 99 percent of the Negroes have remained nonviolent tactically."

When given an opportunity to endorse the negative outlook of the day, Doc goes the other way.

"I refuse to give up," he asserts. "I refuse to despair in this moment. I refuse to allow myself to fall into the dark chambers of pessimism, because I think in any social revolution the one thing that keeps it going is hope, and when hope dies somehow the revolution degenerates into a kind of nihilistic philosophy which says you must engage in disruption for disruption's sake.... I believe that the forces of goodwill, white and black, in this country can work together to bring about a resolution.... We have the resources to do it.... Certainly the Negroes and the decent committed whites — maybe they are in a minority now, but they are there — must work together to so arouse the conscience of this nation."

\* \* \*

Back in Atlanta, "Respect" is the highlight of SCLC's annual banquet on August 14, in the same ballroom where Doc addressed the deejays. This time it isn't a record: it's Aretha herself. She is the hottest singer in the country, who, only last April, was crowned "Queen of Soul" by deejay Pervis "The Blues Man" Spann at the Regal Theater in Chicago.

Doc calls her "Ree." He has known her since she hit the gospel circuit as a thirteen-year-old girl opening the services for her preacher father, wrecking the church with her versions of "There Is a Fountain Filled with Blood" and "Precious Lord." In fact, when in Detroit, Doc stays at the Franklin family home. He takes particular pride in the fact that Aretha is the product of his black Baptist culture and that she, along with Ray Charles, has been able to sanctify the spirit of secular music with the unmistakable glory of God. Among the veteran singers, Mahalia Jackson has a special place in Doc's heart. But this twenty-five-year-old truth-telling Aretha Franklin, her hair piled high on her head, is something else entirely. Doc loves how she brings that black church feeling to the world. Together with the other fourteen hundred people who've come to support SCLC, he's on his feet, clapping his hands to the rhythms of "Ree-ree-ree-ree respect.... Give it to me when I get home."

The three-day convention is notable for the absence of Black Power posters and the presence of banners that say

"Black Is Beautiful." In Doc's presidential address—the last he will give before the only organization he ever founded—he broaches the thorny issue of egotism as it impacts public figures like himself: "What I'm trying to get you to see this morning is that a man may be self-centered in his self-denial and self-righteous in his self-sacrifice. His generosity may feed his ego, and his piety may feed his pride. So without love, benevolence becomes egotism, and martyrdom becomes spiritual pride."

The convention itself is rife with conflict. Arguments over strategy go on for hours, the infighting among SCLC factions more vicious than ever. The drinking is as intense as the disputes. When Bayard Rustin fails to show up for a panel discussion on the ongoing crisis in the ghettoes, Doc takes over and delivers a scathing critique.

"The tragic truth," he says, "is that Congress, more than the American people, is now running wild with racism." Addressing the issue of the growing rage among black Americans, he says he feels that it is "purposeless to tell Negroes they should not be enraged when they should be." When pressed for a solution, his answer is, "Mass civil disobedience can use rage as a constructive and creative force."

The next day the *New York Times* takes his remarks out of context: "Dr. King Planning Protests to 'Dislocate' Large Cities." On the editorial page the paper denounces him for what they called a "formula for discord."

The vague nature of a civil resistance project has the SCLC staff confused. As summer turns to fall, what will

Doc be doing? Working in the Northern ghettoes? Bringing focus to the flagrant inequities that still plague the South? In the face of the recent riots, will his inflammatory rhetoric about the tragically misguided war in Vietnam be muted in order to reestablish his relationship with the administration, as a way to bolster social services?

Decisions must be made. Priorities must be set. The path ahead must be clear. Doc does not have the luxury of hesitation. History is moving with lightning speed. No matter his decision, he will be assaulted by the left, right, or center—or very likely all three. But he must decide.

Within days he is scheduled to fly to Chicago to deliver the opening address to the National Conference for New Politics, a landmark event long in the planning. Some 372 various political groups will be represented, including radical splinter factions on the left.

Ever mindful of Doc's eroding image, Stanley Levison urges him not to attend. It will be undisciplined. It will be a circus. It will reflect badly on Doc's judgment. "What rubs off on you," Levison tells his friend, "is that you are dealing with people who do not know their politics."

Doc deliberates.

Caution says "Stay away."

Doc throws caution to the wind.

*Chapter Nine*

---

# CHAOS

For Doc, loyalty trumps caution. He's unwaveringly loyal to his core beliefs and to the people who have stood with him through thick and thin. Among those are Dr. Benjamin Spock and clergyman William Sloane Coffin, chaplain of Yale University. Both men have pressed him to attend the National Conference for New Politics, the five-day convocation organized by affluent pro–civil rights Harvard instructor Martin Peretz, who wants to use the occasion to promote a King/Spock presidential ticket. Peretz's plans—as well as Spock and Coffin's goal to galvanize antiwar sentiment— prove untenable. From a public relations and policy-making point of view, the conference is an unmitigated disaster. When it is over, Doc realizes that his participation is a major misstep, arming his enemies with even more ammunition with which to attack his standing as a leader with a cohesive constituency.

On August 31, the first day of the convocation, he has high hopes. Riding over to Chicago's Coliseum to deliver the keynote address to three thousand delegates, he reviews his notes. He will advocate supporting democratic revolutions around the world. Once again he will make the case for an immediate American pullout from Vietnam. He will avoid what he calls "the hate Johnson" thing. He will take the high road.

In essence, though, he will not be heard. The minute he steps out of the car, he realizes that the mood is against him. The mood reflects more than anger. Rage is in the air. Escorted into the Coliseum, Doc's heart sinks as he hears the cries from a group of black militants: "Kill whitey! Kill whitey!" Everywhere he looks he sees placards that read "Down with nonviolence!" and "Make way for Rap Brown!"

At the podium, he tries to bend the mood from mindless indignation to thoughtful reason. His hope is that by lucidly restating his unequivocal opposition to the war he will strike a common chord with the great assemblage. "No war in our history has been so violative of our conscience and national interests," he says, "and so destructive of our moral standing."

But this time Doc's rhetoric falls flat. Worse than ignored, he is heckled. Young black delegates stand up and shout derisive insults. Others, bored by his long declamation, get up and walk out. He is mocked, disregarded, and, at best, merely tolerated. Later he tells Levison that the experience was "awful.... The black nationalists gave me trouble. They kept interrupting me, kept yelling things at me." One official report from the Chicago Police Department describes Doc as "afraid, worried and tired."

Defeated in his attempt to unify the warring factions, he leaves Chicago for Washington the next morning, skipping the rest of the convocation. The National Conference for New Politics becomes a tragic symbol of trouble on the left. According to the *Chicago Tribune,* it turns into "a maelstrom as communication failed between Negroes and whites who came here to attend what was described as a third national political convention." *The New Yorker* calls it "a travesty of radical politics at work." The *New York Times* headline reads, "Whites and Negroes Split at New Politics Parley."

At one point three hundred black delegates leave the meetings at the Palmer House Hotel and occupy the Hyde Park Methodist Church. There are threats: if the white minister and white visitors do not leave, the group will burn down the building. Back at the Palmer House, whites are refused entry to H. Rap Brown's speech in which he declares, "We should take lessons in violence from the honkies." At another session in the hotel ballroom, two women seeking to increase female participation are shouted down and forbidden to speak.

Even for James Bevel, perhaps SCLC's most outspoken radical, the militants' mercilessness is too much. He calls them "masochistic fascists" and takes at face value the threats against his life because of his disagreement with the convention's anti-Israel opposition.

As the madness plays out in Chicago, Doc realizes that not only has the conference failed to meet its goal—to unify the leftist political forces—but, even worse, it has demonstrated to a national audience that those forces are at one another's throats. The dialogue between liberals and radicals has broken down. Mistrust between black and white activists has reached an alarming level. And the Negro-Jewish America coalition, one of the strongest hallmarks of the civil rights movement, is in shambles.

Doc is especially disturbed at this latest development, manifest in the thirteen-point policy statement issued at the end of the National Conference for New Politics. It was only the adoption of this statement—without a single word changed—that, according to the *New York Times,* "kept 400 Negro delegates from deserting the radical gathering....The most controversial section of the policy statement drafted by the so-called Black Caucus put the convention on record as condemning 'the imperialistic Zionist war' between Israel and the Arab states."

Out of both personal conviction and the practical need to shore up his coalition with Jewish supporters, Doc later writes to Morris Abram, president of the American Jewish Committee, stating, "The staff members of SCLC who attended the conference were the most vigorous and articulate opponents of the simplistic resolution on the Middle East....It is not only that anti-Semitism is immoral—though that alone is enough. It is used to divide Negro and Jew, who have effectively collaborated in the struggle for justice."

After this calamitous Labor Day weekend in Chicago, that collaboration will never be the same.

As doubts grow about Doc's relevance as an effective public figure, his friends worry about his mental health. No one close to him can fail to see his despondency. When Clarence Jones, one of Doc's chief counselors, has dinner in New York City at the home of Dr. Arthur Logan, Doc's personal physician, the topic is the emotional welfare of their close friend. Logan and his wife, Marian, are convinced that Doc's bouts with depression are more serious and frequent than ever before.

"I'm going to recommend that Doc see a psychiatrist," Logan tells Jones. "I'm going to strongly urge him to seek counseling."

"I know your intentions are good," says Jones, "but your words will be wasted."

"Why do you say that? After all, I'm a physician offering him a professional opinion and the name of another highly respected physician. Surely he'll give this serious thought. Surely he'll respond."

"He won't," Jones says.

"How can you be so sure?"

"I know the man. I know his heart."

"And what in his heart will keep him from neglecting his mental health? Doc is sophisticated enough to realize psychotherapy has nothing to do with any emotional or moral shortcoming."

"Of course he realizes that," says Clarence. "But his greater realization is that, given the FBI surveillance into every aspect of his life, any psychiatric treatment will be used to further besmirch his character. That, in turn, will hurt the movement. The movement is his heart. He'll do nothing to injure the movement."

Doc will not be seeing a shrink anytime soon.

Years later, there will be speculation by various psychiatrists that Doc's "brief depressive episodes" likely contributed to his sense of radical empathy for the suffering of others.

Ironically, the very day after being heckled during his keynote address to the National Conference for New Politics, he is standing before the American Psychological Association in Washington, DC, delivering a major paper: "The Role of the Behavioral Scientist in the Civil Rights Movement."

He is relieved that this audience, as opposed to the fiery radicals he faced in Chicago, regards him respectfully. For the most part they are academics. He delivers a long and learned disquisition on the need for white intellectuals to understand the psychological underpinnings of black rage. He quotes the nineteenth-century French writer Victor Hugo: "If the soul is left in darkness, sins will be committed. The guilty one is not he who commits the sin, but the one who causes the darkness." He references black psychologist Kenneth Clark, who "has said that Negroes are moved by a suicide instinct in riots and Negroes know there is a tragic truth in this observation. Social scientists should also disclose the suicide instinct that governs the administration and Congress in their total failure to respond constructively."

Always the preacher, Doc struggles to conclude on an inspiring note. This time his tone is tentative: "We may be able to emerge from the bleak and desolate midnight of man's inhumanity to man, into the bright and glittering daybreak of freedom and justice.

"I have not lost hope. I must confess that these have been very difficult days for me personally. And these have been difficult days for every civil rights leader, for every lover of justice and peace."

Flying from Washington to Atlanta, Doc knows that far more difficult days lie ahead. It is one thing to reflect upon the ever-widening cracks in his longtime coalition with white liberals. Even more urgent, though, is a need to repair the deep divisions threatening to rip apart SCLC. There is also the chronic problem of finances. Fund-raising has always been a challenge, but with the marked decrease in Doc's prestige as a national leader, money is tighter than ever.

For five days in mid-September, Doc will be at the Airlie Center, a retreat located in the Piedmont foothills in Warrenton, Virginia, an hour's drive from Washington. Once again, the staff will meet to reexamine the recent past and plan the future. Once again, it will be something of a nightmare.

Before he leaves for Virginia he confesses to Atlanta newspapermen, "I'm tired now. I've been in this thing thirteen years now and I'm really tired."

Doc is deeply familiar with 1 John 4:18, which says,

"Perfect love casts out fear," but there is no doubt that during this season of his life fear is there. Fear, in fact, is the subject of a sermon he preaches at Ebenezer two days before he leaves for the retreat. In addressing the issue, Doc is true to form: he personalizes his preaching, using the pulpit to work through his own internal struggles.

"We often develop inferiority complexes," he tells the church, "and we stumble through life with a feeling of insecurity, a lack of self-confidence, and a sense of impending failure.... A fear of what life may bring encourages some persons to wander aimlessly along the frittering road of excessive drink and sexual promiscuity."

The sermon has a confessional feeling as he speaks of dark moments in his own life, times when he was afraid. It's his faith in God that lets him overcome fear. "I know this," he says. "I know it from my own personal experiences."

His personal experience as head of SCLC has never been more difficult. The Airlie Center retreat is rife with discord.

Jesse Jackson wants to focus on local movements like the one he leads in Chicago. Harry Wachtel, a Wall Street lawyer, questions the efficacy of Jackson's Operation Breadbasket. Jackson, in turn, says he will not listen to the remarks of a "slave master." Doc tries to keep Jesse cool, but the heat only rises.

Hosea Williams argues that emphasis must be brought back to civil rights and activities in the South.

Ralph Abernathy and Andrew Young insist that the

organization concentrate on poverty. Doc agrees. He likes the idea of sit-ins at the office of labor secretary W. Willard Wirtz to protest unemployment among the poor.

But always-passionate James Bevel counters that the poverty campaign is little more than "bus fare next to a misguided war."

None of this matters, argues the finance committee, because none of this will happen until SCLC, on the verge of bankruptcy, is brought to solvency. More than SCLC's simply lacking funds for current and future activities, there is also the matter of mounting debts. Ironically, there are past-due legal bills incurred during these many years when Doc has taken moral stances against unjust laws.

Doc says he'll find the money. He'll recruit his loyal showbiz buddies like Harry Belafonte to do a tour of fund-raising concerts at which they'll entertain and he'll make remarks. The tour is certain to bring in considerable cash.

The finance people say that there are no certainties when it comes to fund-raising. Money is needed immediately.

Doc feels that unity is needed immediately. He wants to unify SCLC to mount a massive campaign this fall and winter to protest the plight of the poor. Poverty is the core issue, the fire that is fueling black rage, the reason that his people, living in the midst of an affluent country spending billions on foreign wars and billions more on trips to outer space, are trapped in a cycle of frustration and despair. Doc's despair was evident when, earlier in the month, he told the convention of psychologists that "the unemployment of Negro youth ranges up to 40 percent in some slums.

The riots are almost entirely youth events—the age range of participants is from 13 to 25. What hypocrisy it is to talk of saving the new generation...while consigning it to unemployment and provoking it to violent alternatives." Decent jobs, equal educational opportunities for the impoverished—these are issues burning within Doc's soul.

Yet his passion cannot override the dissent among the troops. The arguments over priorities go deep into the night. The strengths of the various personalities—Jesse Jackson, James Bevel, Hosea Williams—are on full display. These are forceful, eloquent men whose agendas often clash with Doc's. Sometimes the clashes get to the point where Doc feels utterly powerless. On this particular night, he drinks himself into a fury.

This is the same night that Andy Young has brought Joan Baez to the retreat to voice her views. Baez is adamant about focusing on the war. She wants to convince Doc to put SCLC resources behind massive protests at military bases. Before she can make her presentation, though, she and Andy encounter a nasty confrontation between Doc, Jesse Jackson, and James Bevel. Doc is cursing at the top of his lungs. Tears are streaming down his face. Liquor has fueled his rage. He says that he's had it: He's had it with the fruitless arguments about policies and strategies; he's had it with the pressures; he's had it with trying to manage an unmanageable organization. He screams, "I don't want to do this anymore! I just want to go back to my little church!"

The tumult causes Joan to quickly leave the scene. It's

hardly the right moment for the folk singer to address the minister. Instead, Andy and Ralph ease Doc into his room to sleep it off.

The next morning, nursing a hangover, he is apologetic.

"Well," he tells Baez, "now you must know that I'm not a saint."

"And I'm not the Virgin Mary," says Joan, before adding, "What a relief!"

Relocating his dignity, Doc patiently listens to his senior staff offer conflicting visions of SCLC's immediate future. His temples throb. His head aches. The pain is not merely the result of a hangover, but of the undeniable truth that his truth is not shared by the bulk of his immediate constituency. The only truth about which there is no disagreement is a practical one. Without money, nothing will be accomplished.

Doc realizes that he must rise to the occasion. He must recruit the most glittering stars in his galaxy — perennial favorites like Sammy Davis Jr. and current chart toppers like Aretha Franklin — and mount a tour.

Surely such shows will fill the great arenas of the country and tens of thousands of supporters will attend. Surely these musical rallies will not only bring in desperately needed funds but also provide Doc with a platform to express his heart and do what he has been struggling to do ever since he spoke at the Riverside Church: touch the soul of an ailing nation.

*Chapter Ten*

# OMINOUS CLOUDS

The tour is set. Coast to coast, eight dates over twelve days in October: Oakland, Los Angeles, Houston, Chicago, Cleveland, Washington, Philly, and a grand finale in Boston.

The last great fund-raising effort took place in Europe amid significant controversy. It was March 1966. The government, afraid that Doc would openly oppose the Vietnam War—this was a year before his speech at the Riverside Church—tried to get the humanitarian sponsoring organization to cancel. But actors sympathetic to SCLC—Peter O'Toole, Melina Mercouri, Yves Montand, and Simone Signoret—intervened and secured an even larger venue for the event that would feature a speech by Doc and songs by Belafonte. The U.S. State Department ordered the American ambassador to France not to attend. Even though Doc did criticize the war, he made it clear that this was a personal opinion and not a shift in priorities for his movement.

At the time, vehement war protestors, who were hoping for a stronger stance, were disappointed. They would have to wait another year for his thinking to evolve. Meanwhile, the fund-raiser was a huge success.

Eighteen months later, Doc is desperate for another such success.

The lineup is set. Belafonte is on the bill. Aretha will appear at three of the shows. Sidney Poitier will speak at two others. Joan Baez has committed, along with the comic Nipsey Russell. Jazz great Dizzy Gillespie will be playing in Boston.

Hopes are high. And then, on opening night in Oakland, hopes are dashed.

The audience barely fills one-fourth of the Coliseum. When Harry Belafonte and Sammy Davis appear, it is bad enough that their songs seem out-of-date and irrelevant to the current soul music culture. But from the stage Sammy begins to speak about the importance of the civil rights movement *not* venturing from civil rights. He doesn't like this antiwar business and wants to talk about his upcoming trip to Vietnam to entertain the troops. When Joan Baez appears, she argues the opposite, urging Sammy to tell the soldiers to come home. She vows that tomorrow she and other protestors will block the entrances to the Armed Forces Induction Center, right there in Oakland. By the time Doc makes his remarks, it is clear that, even during a fund-raising concert, he cannot control the warring factions among his own troops.

The next day Baez is arrested along with 123 other

demonstrators and sentenced to ten days in jail, thus keeping her off the rest of the tour.

In Los Angeles, a city known to support liberal causes, the crowd is thin and the event marred by a bomb threat causing an evacuation and long delay.

Houston is worse. Black state legislator Curtis Graves, in charge of promoting the concert, meets with Doc at the Shamrock Hilton a few hours before showtime and tells him that for an auditorium that holds four thousand, only five hundred tickets have been sold.

"We're going to look bad, Doc," he says. "What should we do?"

Rather than answer, Doc goes into prayer. For some fifteen minutes, Graves listens to Doc commune with God. When the prayer is over, Doc says, "Give away the tickets."

Graves does just that. A couple of hours later, when Graves is arranging to give away tickets at supermarkets, a limo pulls up. A black chauffeur emerges.

"Who's in charge?" asks the chauffeur.

"I am," Graves answers.

"This is for your boss," he says, handing over an envelope.

"Who is it from?"

"My boss."

"Who's your boss?" asks Graves.

"Doesn't matter. He doesn't want to say. He doesn't even want any tickets. Just wants your boss to have this."

Graves opens the envelope holding ten thousand dollars.

That's the good news. The bad news is that during the

concert itself stink bombs are set off. The audience is holding handkerchiefs to their eyes and noses. Belafonte takes the stage and defiantly says, "I was told that if I came to Houston, I would fare no better than John F. Kennedy did in Dallas." The show goes on. Aretha sings "Respect."

Aretha's appearances with Doc and Belafonte in Cleveland and Washington do not increase sales. Business is so bleak that Doc is forced to send a telegram to supporters in Philly, his next stop: "We urgently need a commitment from your organization for a block of 300 tickets," he writes. "Prices are $7.50, $5.50 and $4.50."

Seeing that Doc is reeling from the disastrous tour, Dora McDonald, his secretary in Atlanta, urges Stanley Levison to speak to her boss. "Dr. King has been so despondent over how badly the concerts have been going," she says, "that he can't bring himself to do a thing."

Beyond failing to bring in money, the tour struggles to earn back its costs.

A bit of much-needed good news arrives when, in the midst of the tour, an all-white jury in Mississippi convicts seven white men for the 1964 murders of civil rights workers James Chaney, Andrew Goodman, and Michael Schwerner.

"I am pleasantly surprised," Doc tells the Associated Press. "The decision represents a first step on a thousand-mile journey toward the goal of equal administration of justice in Mississippi."

Doc does not attend the massive antiwar rally on October 21, during which fifty-five thousand protestors march on the Pentagon—a cataclysmic event later immortalized in Norman Mailer's book *The Armies of the Night*—but he is in the nation's capital the next day. He has come to speak at another poorly attended fund-raising concert after testifying before the LBJ-appointed Kerner Commission, which is looking to identify the root causes of the recent riots. Defiantly, Doc calls for "escalating non-violence" and, in his remarks to waiting reporters, ups the ante by saying, "The time has come if we can't get anything done otherwise to camp right here in Washington...just camp here and stay here by the thousands and thousands."

The *Washington Post* rebukes Doc's remarks as "a call to anarchy."

A week later, on October 30, a dark and rainy day, he goes to prison in Alabama along with his brother, A. D.; Ralph Abernathy; and his longtime trusted aide Wyatt Tee Walker, all of whom participated in the 1963 civil rights demonstration in Birmingham that the courts have upheld as illegal.

"It is with mixed emotions that I return to Birmingham," Doc tells the press, "to serve this five-day sentence for insisting upon our right to peacefully protest the brutal and unconstitutional treatment of Negroes in this city....I have been happy to enter the jails for the freedom of my people....But I am sad that the Supreme Court...could not uphold the rights of individual citizens in the face of deliberate use of the courts of the State of Alabama as a means of oppression....Perhaps these five days will afford me an opportunity for a more intense and serious evaluation of our situation, for all the signs of our time indicate that this is a dark hour in the life of America. Our jailing is but symptomatic of the ominous clouds which overshadow our national destiny."

Walking into his jail cell with three books—the Bible, an economics text, and *The Confessions of Nat Turner,* the recently published William Styron novel about the 1831 Virginia slave revolt—Doc's intention is to write a sequel to his celebrated "Letter from Birmingham Jail." He's determined to work through his exhaustion and commit his thoughts to paper.

Concerned about his safety, officials move him from one jail to another, and he falls sick with the flu. When Coretta and Juanita Abernathy visit their husbands, they remark to reporters that not only are the facilities subpar in terms of decent food and adequate health services, but they are also, ironically, still segregated.

Racked by chills and a hacking cough, Doc tries to write but doesn't get far. He reads over what he has already said in a formal statement before entering prison—a reflection on the reason he is here. "Today we return to a Birmingham jail once again to bear witness, this time against a weapon which has the potential of doing greater harm to America than [Birmingham Commissioner of Public Safety] Bull Connor's dogs. . . . The weapon is the 'X-party injunction' used by hostile local courts to frustrate and silence the vital First Amendment rights. . . . We are witnessing an escalating disregard for constitutional freedom. In the last two weeks U.S. Marshals, state troopers and local police have clubbed demonstrators in Washington, Berkeley and Madison, Wis.; police have dragged girls by the hair in Brooklyn, tear gas has scattered and routed protesters in Washington, Berkeley, and Oberlin, Ohio, and even the odious fire hoses of Bull Connor were callously deployed against college students at Oberlin. . . . We call out to America: 'Take heed. Do not allow the Bill of Rights to become a prisoner of war.' "

He picks up pen again to fight through the fever and write what he envisions as a "Bill of Rights for the Disadvantaged," a new version of the GI Bill (of Rights), the 1944 law granting special benefits to World War II veterans. But his sick body and disheartened mind overwhelm his ambition. In the isolation of his cell he can do little but suffer.

He emerges from prison on November 5, still weak but determined to reenter the fray. After a quick trip to Atlanta to see Coretta and the kids, enjoy a home-cooked meal, and sleep in his own bed, he's off to Cleveland, where he hopes to celebrate the victory of Carl Stokes, campaigning to be the first Negro mayor of a major American city. Over the past year, Doc has flown into Cleveland on a regular basis and tirelessly bolstered voter registration drives. This is the same city where Doc even tried to get prostitutes to register and vote. On election night, he and Ralph Abernathy meet with Stokes in their room in the hotel where the campaign is headquartered. The candidate assures Doc that, should he win, he'll call for him to join the celebration.

Later that evening Stokes does win in a close contest.

It is a landmark moment in American electoral politics. Doc is gratified to have played a major role in turning out a massive black vote. After a long and difficult battle, he looks forward to standing beside the mayor-elect in the glow of this hard-earned victory. But after the final returns are announced and the TV cameras focus on a smiling Stokes waving to his cheering supporters in the crowded ballroom, Doc is nowhere to be seen. Stokes has reneged on his promise to have Doc join him onstage. Looking to broaden his appeal to the nonblack constituency, Stokes is convinced that his association with Doc — who remains controversial and, in the minds of many, increasingly irrelevant — will do him no good. Doc is crushed.

He puts his personal feelings aside, though, when he addresses the press about the victory of Stokes as well as that of Richard Hatcher, a black American who on this same night in November has been elected mayor of Gary, Indiana. "These victories," Doc says, "represent a new political fervor among America's Negro citizens.... This surge of political action is a desperation quest to find someone to champion the cause of the poor and oppressed in our cities.... New resources must come from the business community and from Washington or we have only set up two outstanding men as lambs for the slaughter."

In the face of this humiliating rejection by Stokes, Doc is once again generous to a fault. But then he turns up the heat, focusing on the issue closest to his heart — in the words of Jesus, "the least of these my brethren":

"Even as I speak, the stage is being set in the Congress

and at the White House for an immoral and monumental backward step in our nation's War on Poverty.... I am appalled that there is a serious possibility that the House may eliminate this week 272,000 of our nation's poor children from Head Start programs; 250,000 high school dropouts from the Neighborhood Youth Corps and an additional 50,000 poor adults from much-needed jobs. To cut the program in this fashion is an open invitation to violence and social disorder in the streets of our beleaguered urban ghettoes. It is disgraceful that Congress can vote upwards of 35 billion dollars a year for senseless immoral war in Vietnam, but cannot vote a weak 2.5 billion dollars to carry on our all too feeble efforts to bind up the wounds of our nation's 32 million poor. This is nothing short of Congress engaging in political guerrilla warfare against the defenseless poor of our nation."

In the aftermath of the victories of Stokes and Hatcher, Doc talks to his aides about the meaninglessness of black faces in high places if these Negro public officials cannot galvanize the power of government — on both the local and the national level — for an out-and-out assault on poverty.

Poverty is one issue that won't go away; the war is another.

On Monday, November 13, preparing for still another trip — this one to England to accept an honorary degree from the University of Newcastle upon Tyne — Doc reads a story in the *Atlanta Journal-Constitution* that raises his spirits, if only for a moment. The day before, seated on the

first pew in a historic church in Colonial Williamsburg—
the same pew on which George Washington once sat—
Lyndon Johnson is read the riot act by a white clergyman,
surely influenced by Doc's gospel-based antiwar stance.
Reverend Cotesworth Pinckney Lewis unapologetically
uses the pulpit of his Episcopal church to condemn the
president's policy in Vietnam.

Poverty, militarism. And when he boards his transat-
lantic flight and settles in his seat, Doc peruses the special
issue of *Newsweek* devoted to the third great matter that,
to paraphrase the poet John Keats, haunts his days and
chills his dreaming nights: the crisis of race in America.

As the jet taxis down the runway and prepares for take-
off, Doc straps on his seat belt, girds himself for another
long ride, and, as is his nature, engages in deep reflection.

He has been addressing the issue of racism since he
began preaching at the Dexter Avenue Baptist Church in
Montgomery in the fifties.

He was hammering away at the issue of war well before
his speech at the Riverside Church some seven months ago.

And in the aftermath of the riots of this past summer and
the reactionary politics of Congress, he's convinced more
than ever that the issue of poverty must be prioritized.

Like a malignant cancer, poverty is eating at the very
soul of black America.

Poverty is threatening our very democracy. It's now a
matter of national security.

This is the essence of his spiritual rebirth and recommitment to the gospel of Christ.

The Bible, the book that Doc loves best, speaks about poverty in Lamentations: "The tongue of the nursing infant sticks to the roof of its mouth for thirst; the children beg for food, but no one gives to them."

Consumed by war and racial rancor, America is not giving.

Despite his own battle with political and personal despondency, Doc realizes that he is morally obligated to muster all his energy to bring attention to the poor. Their suffering cannot be rendered invisible.

As he flies over the dark Atlantic into the cold night, he would like to take an easier course — a sabbatical, perhaps; a cushy job in a think tank; the presidency of a quiet college in New England — but he can't. His conscience won't allow it. In this winter of his discontent, he forges on.

## Chapter Eleven

# "I, MARTIN LUTHER KING, TAKE THEE, NON-VIOLENCE, TO BE MY WEDDED WIFE"

It's another verbal slugfest, another contentious SCLC conference in Frogmore, South Carolina.

It's the same old story—only this time it's worse. Among Doc's supporters, the disenchantment is deepening and Doc's lieutenants are fighting to take the campaign in different directions. James Bevel is unrestrained and long-winded in his opposition to redirecting SCLC efforts to address poverty. Backing Bevel, Jesse Jackson leaves early on a fund-raising trip that Doc suspects will serve Jesse's ambitions to start a splinter group of his own. Hosea Williams fiercely attacks Doc's choice for the new SCLC executive director: William Rutherford, a Chicago Negro with a PhD from the Sorbonne, who has lived in Europe for well over a decade.

"That nigger don't know nothing about niggers!" Williams screams in Doc's face.

Even before Frogmore, Doc faced another roadblock, during a meeting with Olympic athletes who would be competing in the 1968 Summer Olympic Games. They wanted to use the event to dramatize their stance against racism. Doc wanted to help them formulate a plan, but it was no use. For now, Black Power militants undermined the prospect of the athletes conducting a peaceful protest — though this does turn out to be the Olympic Games at which John Carlos and Tommie Smith hold up their black-gloved fists.

In this moment, militancy and violence — all the rage among the avant-garde black activists during the winter of 1967 — are increasingly on Doc's mind.

"The riots are now in the center of the stage," he says. "Some Negroes argue that they are the incipient forms for rebellion and guerrilla tactics that will be the feature of the Negro revolt."

He argues long and hard against the efficacy of this approach while pointing to its moral bankruptcy. He realizes that the political currents are against him. He tells a story about flying from New York to London in 1956 on a propeller plane. The trip took more than nine-and-a-half hours, but the return flight was three hours longer. Doc asked the pilot why. "When we leave New York," said the captain, "a strong tail wind is in our favor, but when we return a strong head wind is against us." The pilot added, "Don't worry, these four engines are capable of battling the winds."

"In any social revolution," Doc tells his dissatisfied troops, "there are times when the tail winds of triumph and fulfillment favor us, and other times when strong head winds of disappointment and setbacks beat against us relentlessly. We must not permit adverse winds to over- whelm us as we journey across life's Atlantic. We must be sustained by...engines of courage.... This refusal to be stopped, this courage to be, this determination to go on in spite of, is the hallmark of great movements....

"I've decided that, on this question of non-violence, I'm going to stand by it. I'm going to love because it's just lovely to love. I'm going to be non-violent because I believe it is the answer to mankind's problems. I'm not going to bargain with reality.... I've taken a vow — I, Martin Luther King, take thee, non-violence, to be my wedded wife, for better or for worse, for richer or for poorer...in sickness and in health, until death do us part."

Doc sets out his plan for a series of rallies, sit-ins, and encampments to protest poverty — a Poor People's Campaign — that will start in Washington. "If we will do this," he says, "we will be able to turn this nation upside down and right side up, and...cry out that we are children of God, made in his image. This will be a glorious day; at that moment the morning stars will sing together, and the souls of God will shout for joy."

Doc's staff members, though, are not shouting for joy.

They continue to question the likelihood of signing up three thousand nonviolent volunteers to join the protest.

"I'm serious about this," Doc replies. "I'm on fire about this thing."

When his aides' doubts keep coming, Doc keeps firing back. He talks about Peter being fired up for Jesus on the day of Pentecost, when his sermon converted three thousand souls. He talks about concentration camp survivors who clung to hope; baseball teams that pulled out a victory in the bottom of the ninth; a violinist who, having snapped his A string, found a way to transpose the composition midperformance. He cites the Book of Revelation: "Strengthen what remains and is about to die, for I have found your deeds unfinished in the sight of my God."

Doc feels compelled to finish his work.

"We've gone for broke before," he declares, "but not in the way we're going this time. If necessary I'm going to stay in jail six months."

When the conference is over, the *New York Times* quotes Doc about his plans for "massive civil disobedience," which are to include "mass sit-ins inside and at the gate of factories and thousands of unemployed youths camping in Washington as the bonus marchers did in the thirties....I am convinced civil disobedience can curtail riots." He expects whites to join in the protests.

It is the issue of Vietnam, though, not the issue of poverty, or nonviolent solutions, that continues to attract the vast majority of the country's attention.

At the end of November, Eugene McCarthy, a Democratic senator from Minnesota, beats Bobby Kennedy to the punch by announcing his candidacy in the presidential primaries. McCarthy's anti-Johnson crusade is centered on a single issue: opposition to LBJ's war. In the autumn of 1967, the story of Doc's Poor People's Campaign is buried by the increasingly heated contest within the Democratic Party to oust their seated president.

On the orders of his physician, Doc takes a short break during the first week of December. He flies to Bimini, in the Bahamas, for a few days of relaxation, and he is invited to the home of Adam Clayton Powell, who, due to budgetary mismanagement of the House committee that he chairs, had been excluded from the Ninetieth Congress, only to win a special election in his Harlem district. His legal status uncertain, Powell has decided to stay in Bimini indefinitely.

Dinner with Powell does little to relax Doc. The congressman spends the evening making disparaging remarks at Doc's expense. According to Powell, not only is America going to hell in a handbasket, but the Negro people no longer have a leader they can admire. Doc is fooling himself if he thinks he still makes a difference; Doc should wake up to the facts and admit that this nonviolence business is obsolete. His movement has failed; no one takes SCLC seriously anymore. The militants have won over the heart of the people, and the militants are right. No movement can succeed without exerting physical power. Violence is necessary. Any fool knows that to be true.

Realizing that any attempt to counter Powell's arguments would fall on deaf ears, Doc just sits and listens. The congressman likes bullying his guest. He enjoys dishing out insults. At the head of the long dining room table, the black prince in exile speaks with unwavering authority on all matters, especially the precipitous decline in Doc's national status.

Doc deftly ignores the taunting. After all, he's on vacation. He's come to the Bahamas to relax, not argue. But Powell is persistent, gung ho about getting his guest to admit that his Gandhi-like approach to social change has run its course. Doc will admit no such thing. He simply smiles, gets up from the table, and walks to the veranda. The sky is ablaze with stars. The sea sparkles with moonlight. Night-blooming flowers scent the air. Back in the dining room, Powell is still pontificating. In the darkness, standing alone, Doc seeks peace.

*Chapter Twelve*

# IRONIC ANNIVERSARY

The respite is quick. Doc is back in America, back to the grind.

There are a number of speaking engagements, but the most meaningful one is on December 10 in Montgomery. He is invited to deliver a Sunday sermon at the ninetieth anniversary of the Dexter Avenue Baptist Church, his original pastorate. The trip to Alabama is awash in nostalgia. This is, after all, where it all began.

Driving through the city on his way to the sanctuary, Doc is startled to see hooded members of the Ku Klux Klan assembled in front of the state capitol. They are preparing a Sunday morning rally. Doc can only sigh.

Everything has changed, yet nothing has changed.

He thinks back a dozen years to his arrival in Alabama. The Montgomery Improvement Association was struggling to find a leader among the city's black clergy for its impending citywide bus boycott. Many of the older preachers were reluctant to take on the task. Others lacked the skill. Because Doc, at twenty-six, was a fresh face unsullied by hardball city politics, he was viewed as a prime candidate to lead the charge. At first he declined, just as he had similarly withdrawn his name for presidency of the local NAACP. Coretta had recently given birth to Yolanda, their first child. Doc wanted to relish the role of fatherhood and dedicate himself to the spiritual needs of his congregation.

Yet in spite of his initial instinct to tell the boycott organizers no, his conscience compelled him to say yes. That "yes" changed his life and led to a seemingly endless series of brutal challenges that both tested and bolstered his character. The boycott met with not only fierce opposition but imprisonment and threats to his life. When he realized the enormity of the task he had undertaken—and the dangers that it posed to his wife and baby daughter—he wanted to give up. He later rejoiced that he hadn't, and after a year the Montgomery movement succeeded in integrating the citywide bus system.

But that was then. This is now.

Now he drives past the Klan and, only a few blocks later, arrives at the Dexter Avenue Baptist Church, where he is warmly greeted. He takes his seat in the pulpit beside the elders and, waiting to deliver his sermon, smiles at the memory of the moment when it all turned around—when, back in the days of the boycott, his "no" turned to "yes" and resignation transformed into resolution.

Those were crazy, frightening times. Events surrounding the boycott had turned chaotic. He fought for clarity and composure but found himself overwhelmed by uncertainty. He couldn't think, couldn't sleep, couldn't stop worrying.

On one such restless evening he was at home in bed with Coretta when the phone rang. Who was calling at midnight?

"Nigger," said the caller, "we are tired of you and your mess now. And if you aren't out of this town in three days, we're going to blow your brains out and blow up your house."

Doc's heart beat wildly. It was more than fear; it was terror. He couldn't get to sleep. He went into the kitchen to get some coffee. What he really wanted to do was run into the arms of his father and mother, but they were back in Atlanta. He wanted to run back to the university in Boston, where the world seemed more tolerant. He wanted out. He wanted safety. Like Jesus in the garden of Gethsemane, he wanted anything but to walk this dark and dangerous path before him.

So he did what Jesus did: he prayed.

"Lord, I'm down here trying to do what's right. I think I'm right; I think the cause that we represent is right. But Lord, I must confess that I'm weak now; I'm faltering; I'm losing my courage. And I can't let the people see me like this because if they see me weak and losing my courage, they will begin to get weak."

Then the miracle.

The Holy Spirit spoke to his soul and said, "Martin Luther, stand up for righteousness, stand up for justice, stand up for truth. And lo I will be with you, even until the end of the world."

Those words are the strength that has sustained him for these twelve tumultuous years. Yet even as Doc prepares to come to the podium to speak love, the Klansmen, led by Grand Dragon James Spears, eviscerate opponents of the Vietnam War and advocates of gun control while mocking the name of "Martin Lucifer King," just a few blocks away.

Nothing has changed, yet everything has changed.

Twelve years ago when he arrived in Alabama, the civil rights movement was an unrealized dream. Segregation was ironclad. Now legal segregation is gone. Discriminatory voting restrictions are gone. But the cost has been huge. Lives have been lost—Medgar Evers, freedom riders, innocent children. The honors have been unexpected: Doc's picture on the cover of *Time* magazine, being named the youngest recipient of the Nobel Peace Prize, gaining unprecedented access to presidents and prime ministers, recognition as an international figure.

The timing of the Klan rally is recognition of another truth: hatred has not gone into hiding. The vicious racist past is alive—right here and now.

When it finally comes time to address the congregation, Doc stays focused on the doubts that plagued him when he first came to Montgomery. In the presence of sinners and saints, he works through his doubts. He speaks to the congregation, even as he speaks to himself.

Our nation is sick with racism. Sick with militarism.

Sick with a system that perpetuates poverty. Some fifty million people are poverty-stricken.

How to find hope in the darkness?

He points to First Corinthians and what he calls Paul's "magnificent trilogy of durability": faith, hope, and love.

Today hope is his concern—what does it mean and how is it maintained?

He draws a distinction between "magic hope" and "realistic hope." "Magic hope is sheer optimism" that somehow things automatically improve. "Realistic hope is based on a willingness to face the risk of failure, and embrace an 'in spite of' quality."

He equates the loss of hope with death. "If you lose hope absolutely you die," he contends. "A hopeless individual is a dead individual.... When you lose hope you lose creativity, you lose rationality.... I was saying to some of my nationalist friends the other day—we were arguing about violence versus non-violence—that the problem is you've lost hope.... He who loses hope makes the ugly beautiful and the beautiful ugly. He who loses hope makes the true false and the false true.... Hope is animated and undergirded by faith and love."

Doc speaks of how hope got black folks through the hell of American history. "More than seventy-five million black people were lost, murdered and died in the midst of that two hundred and some years of slave trading.... Don't ever romanticize slavery. It's one of the darkest and most evil periods in the history of the world. But the Negro is still going and he's going because he never had the disease of 'giveupitis.' He knew somehow that there was an agreement with an eternal power and he'd look out and say, 'You ain't no nigger. You ain't no slave, but you're God's children.'"

Doc turns inward and reflects on his despondency. "Around in Alabama and Mississippi and up in Cleveland and Chicago every now and then I feel discouraged. Living every day under the threat of death, I feel discouraged... feel my work is in vain, but then the Holy Spirit revives my soul again. 'There is a balm in Gilead to make the wounded whole.' And this is the faith. It's the faith that will carry us through the dark days ahead."

Doc has given his final sermon at the Dexter Avenue Baptist Church, and the days ahead are darker than Doc can even imagine. Forces rip apart the country, demons divide his own people, discord gnaws on his own organization—rancor is on the rise.

Rancor resides in the minds of the Klansmen who, as Doc prays for hope, call for violence. That call is echoed by enraged and embittered groups the world over. As 1967 comes to an end, with America raining bombs on North Vietnam, violence is in the air.

In the face of a culture that has less and less interest in his core values, Doc has invoked the God who, as he says, "can make a way out of no way. I know about Him. I know that He can lift you from the fatigue of despair to the buoyancy of hope. I've seen the lightning flash. I've heard the thunder roar. I've felt sin breakers dashing, trying to conquer my soul, but I heard the voice of Jesus saying, 'Fight on.'"

Yet he cannot pretend that in this festive season all is calm, all is bright. He cannot call the impending New Year happy. As never before, the odds are stacked against him. But the odds don't matter. All that matters is fighting on.

"The race is not to the swift, nor the battle to the strong," he reads in the Book of Ecclesiastes.

Scrutinizing the sociopolitical situation, he realizes that in this coming year the battle will worsen. His enemies will be emboldened. He will make grave personal and professional mistakes. He will break down more than once.

He realizes that he will not survive the battle with human strength alone. And that in reaching for divine sustenance, he will experience fear.

Yet he will keep praying, keep planning. He will keep reaching.

# PART II

# THE FINAL SEASON

*The Last Three Months*

## Chapter Thirteen

# THIRTY-NINE

The year begins ominously.

The war is six years old, soon to be the longest in American history — nearly sixteen thousand Americans killed and a hundred thousand wounded so far. Hoping to finally destroy the enemy, in the first month of 1968 President Johnson unleashes an eleven-week bombing attack on North Vietnam.

J. Edgar Hoover renews his own attack, doubling down on his plans to destroy Doc through the FBI's network of paid informers.

Doc's allies Benjamin Spock and William Sloane Coffin are indicted by the Justice Department for helping young men oppose the draft. Infuriated, Doc calls a press conference in which he attacks the indictments, speaks favorably of Eugene McCarthy's campaign to unseat Johnson, and criticizes Bobby Kennedy for being lackluster in his opposition to the war.

Maintaining his furious pace, Doc flies to California to support Joan Baez, still imprisoned in Oakland for blocking the entrance to a military center. After the visit, he addresses the press.

There are tough questions about his relationship to Adam Clayton Powell, who has publicly announced that Martin Luther King Jr. no longer subscribes to nonviolence. Coming on top of the insults he suffered in Bimini, this takes Doc by surprise. With all due respect to the congressman, he unequivocally refutes the statement. Yet in spite of this blatant misrepresentation, Doc sends a gracious letter to Powell, urging him to return to New York, where his leadership is needed. "You beat the white man at his game," Doc writes, "and became a fighting symbol of power."

His aides are astounded that Doc is able to turn the other cheek and offer the congressman such support.

"Radical love," Harry Belafonte will later reflect, "is Doc's great hallmark. Loving those who are twisting your words. Loving those moving against you. Loving those looking to take your spot and undermine your authority. In the end, Doc is not only offering unconditional love, but he's supporting every organization and individual fighting for the liberation of people throughout the globe. He never allows political discourse to overwhelm his revolutionary moral vision."

Doc's next challenge is to sell his vision to SCLC.

He tells the press that tomorrow he's off to Atlanta, where he will give his troops "marching orders to go into fifteen communities where we will be mobilizing people by the thousands for a massive demonstration in Washington on a quest for jobs and income."

His mission at this latest SCLC staff meeting is clear: this time he will finally and firmly establish the fact that his priority is a Poor People's Campaign in the spring, and that his priority will prevail.

But will it? In Atlanta, the staff remains in revolt. Dissent erupts from the get-go. Doc has to deal with the heated resistance of James Bevel and Jesse Jackson, who are, in the words of one of Doc's aides, "competing with him for leadership." The infighting is brutal. At the end of the day, his patience stretched to the limit, Doc is ready to leave. But Andy Young won't allow it. At that moment the staff breaks into a spirited "Happy Birthday!" Typically, Doc's staff would get him a new suit for his natal day. But this year he is lovingly toasted and presented with a couple of gag gifts: a jar of shoestring potatoes (because Doc has complained about the bad food and shoestring policy of the Birmingham prison) and a mug that reads, "We are cooperating with Lyndon Johnson's War on Poverty. Drop coins and bills in the cup."

Doc smiles and expresses earnest gratitude.

On this day — just another rough-and-tumble workday in the life of a minister who cannot stop working — he turns thirty-nine.

At noon the next day, he's back at it, standing before a bevy of reporters to announce the kickoff of his poverty campaign. He envisions armies of protestors encamped in the nation's capital. His tactics are, in his words, "patterned after the bonus marches back in the thirties....The only difference is that this time we aren't going to be run out of Washington."

His plan is vague—only that the campaign will start in the spring. His inability to unify his own troops is obvious. In private, one aide questions his judgment by asking, "What's going to happen when we bring these people to Washington and Stokely's going to be there?" Doc confesses that he harbors doubts but says, "I don't want to psychoanalyze anybody but myself."

After days of debate, all he can tell his staff is, "Just go to Washington." The ambiguities of the plans should not get in their way. The plans for the Montgomery Bus Boycott were also sketchy, but look what happened.

"We got to be fired up ourselves," Doc keeps preaching to the unconverted supporters.

The supporters remain resistant. The wrangling goes on ad infinitum. One workshop on finances and fund-raising is especially long and arduous. Usually a patient listener, Doc is on the verge of losing it. Rather than run the risk of appearing cranky, he excuses himself for a bathroom break. But instead of heading to the men's room, he quietly exits a side door and walks to his car. Feeling like a truant student escaping school, he drives to the home of Dorothy Cotton, a close aide and director of the Citizenship Education Program of SCLC.

Dorothy is surprised to see him at her front door. Why isn't he at the workshop? What's wrong?

"Don't tell anyone," he whispers in a mischievous voice, "but I snuck out. I just couldn't take another minute."

Dorothy understands. She has been to dozens of such meetings herself. She ushers him into the living room, where he sits in a wooden rocking chair painted yellow. Yellow, she points out, is a calming color. Doc could use a little calm.

He agrees. Calm is just what he lacks; calm is just what he needs. He gets to gently rocking and finds the motion calming.

Clarence Jones is right: Doc will never go to a psychiatrist, but in the presence of a trusted friend like Dorothy Cotton, he is able to reflect inwardly and speak of heavy matters weighing on his heart.

He talks about being despondent. He talks about being exhausted. He expresses doubt about the effectiveness of his leadership. He describes his organization's senior staff as "a team of wild horses." He's bone tired of trying to get them to back his agenda. There comes a time when arguments are futile, a time when a man has to see that he's no longer useful. It's obvious that the political climate has turned against him. Why not move on?

"To where?" asks Dorothy.

To England, Doc explains. A church in Great Britain has offered him a pastorate. A prestigious church. A progressive church. A church where he could write and preach and commune with God without the endless strife that has become his increasingly troubled life in America.

Dorothy wonders whether he is serious.

Doc assures her that he is.

She doesn't respond. She realizes that he needs to vent,

needs to express these mounting frustrations, needs to comfort himself with thoughts of an easier life.

But a pastorate in England, like the presidency of a university, is a romantic fantasy. It'll never happen. Sitting in the yellow chair, rocking late into the night, Doc realizes—as does Dorothy—that he will never abandon the struggle.

Those few hours with Dorothy help revive his spirit.

On the following night, January 16, he is back home with Coretta and the children. After a quiet dinner, he turns on the television to watch Johnson's State of the Union address.

The president argues that this war in Vietnam is winnable. He vigorously defends his military strategy and, amid his ambitious plans to address pressing domestic issues, makes a point of underscoring the threat of urban crime. "The American people," he says, "have had enough of rising crime and lawlessness in this country."

Beyond being disappointed that LBJ shows no inclination to reverse his disastrous military course, Doc hears "crime and lawlessness" as code words for unrest in the black ghettoes. He worries about white backlash and wonders if Johnson is fueling new fire.

Fewer than twenty-four hours pass before Doc picks up the newspaper and is captivated by an incident at the White House that's causing a furor.

The day after the State of the Union address, Lady Bird

Johnson hosts a Women Doers' Luncheon at the White House. Arranged by the first lady's social secretary, the event brings together distinguished women involved in social causes. The topic at hand is how to deal with the rising tide of crime.

Among those guests is Eartha Kitt, the Negro singer, actress, and political activist. Uncomfortable sitting through the innocuous speeches, she bristles when President Johnson himself makes a surprise appearance and a few facile remarks about how crime fighting should be left to the states, not the federal government.

Before LBJ can get away, Eartha confronts him: "But what do we do about delinquent parents, the parents who have to work, for instance, who can't spend the time with their children as they should?"

Social Security provides for day care, Johnson says. He dismisses her by adding, "I think that is a very good question for you to ask yourselves, you women here, and you all tell me what you think."

With that, he rushes out of the room.

There is more talk, more platitudes spoken by respectable women voicing their fears over the spread of lawlessness across the land.

When Lady Bird finally entertains questions from the floor, Eartha immediately raises her hand. This is the moment she has been waiting for.

Eartha lets loose. In plain language, she lets the first lady know that she has "lived in the gutters" and knows what she's talking about. She says that anger in the cities can be traced back to anger over the war, "a war going on that Americans do not understand." She talks about young men "being snatched away from their mothers and being sent off to Vietnam....I am talking as a mother who has a child... so I know the feeling of having a baby coming out of my guts, particularly when it's a boy.... You take the best of the country and send them off to a war and they get shot."

Shocked and offended by this outburst of emotion, the first lady tries to mount a defense. Along with the other women in the room, she is outraged by the effrontery. There are tears in her eyes.

When the luncheon is over, the ladies gather around Lady Bird in solidarity, expressing their regret that their lovely luncheon has been marred by such rudeness. Meanwhile, Eartha leaves the White House alone. Among the many ladies in attendance, she doesn't have a single supporter.

After reading the account, Doc jumps to her defense. This is a woman after his own heart. Hers is the kind of courage that he respects. He makes a point of telling the *New York Times* that he considers Eartha's remarks "appropriate both as to content and place" while finding her comments to the first lady "a very proper gesture."

He personally calls Eartha to say that she's made him proud. In short, Doc is delighted that a strong independent woman from the black community is giving the Johnsons hell.

Doc is drawn to strong independent women. And in January 1968, Doc's relationship with his wife, the strongest woman in his life, is—like everything else—under tremendous strain.

*Chapter Fourteen*

# CONFESSION

Coretta is not happy. While Doc is crisscrossing the country, she is most often alone at home with their four children. She has repeatedly asked him to provide her with a housekeeper, but he has refused. Given his calling as a preacher and advocate for the poor, he feels that they must live modestly. There's also the question of his unwillingness to provide for their children's futures. The Kings' personal finances mirror the finances of SCLC. They barely scrape by.

The larger question is Coretta's role in the movement. She wants to travel and speak more. Two days before Eartha confronted the Johnsons, Coretta was in Washington with a silent brigade of five thousand women who walked through the snow to protest U.S. involvement in Vietnam. She was among the elite group who entered the Capitol to present the official antiwar petition to members of Congress.

Yet when it comes to Coretta's high profile involvement, Doc isn't always enthusiastic.

"Martin has very traditional ideas about women," Coretta says. She struggles to make him understand that she cannot sublimate her own calling to serve. In 1966 she told the press that "not enough attention has been focused on the roles played by women in the struggle. By and large, men have formed the leadership...but...[w]omen have been the backbone of the whole civil rights movement."

Doc cannot disagree. But he also cannot deny his deep ambivalence. Part of Doc wishes that she would simply stay home and care for the children. But another part appreciates the acuity of her intellect and the vital role that she has played in his moral and political growth.

It was Coretta who spent long hours discussing Gandhi with Doc. She understood both the spiritual and the practical properties of nonviolence. Without her encouragement he might have abandoned its principles. In fact, there was a time when he came close to doing just that.

It was during those frightening days in Montgomery. In 1956, the King family home had been bombed. Coretta and the kids had escaped injury, but the trauma remained. Supporters, including Daddy King, urged Doc to hire armed guards. Shaken to the core, Doc applied for a license and bought a gun. It was Coretta who helped persuade him to give up the weapon.

"I reconsidered," Doc would later say. "How could I serve as one of the leaders of a nonviolent movement and at the same time use weapons of violence for my personal protection? Coretta and I talked the matter over for several days and finally agreed that arms were no solution.... We tried to satisfy our friends by having floodlights mounted around the house, and hiring unarmed watchmen around the clock.... I was much more afraid in Montgomery when I had a gun in my house. When I decided that I couldn't keep a gun, I came face-to-face with the question of death and I dealt with it. From that point on, I no longer needed a gun nor have I been afraid. Had we become distracted by the question of my safety we would have lost the moral offensive and sunk to the level of our oppressors."

Coretta emboldened him. But then again, she always had.

When he met her in 1951 he was immediately smitten. He was a twenty-two-year-old student working on his PhD at Boston University's School of Theology. She was a great beauty, a brilliant twenty-three-year-old graduate of prestigious Antioch College and a voice student at the New England Conservatory. Within weeks, Doc was telling his family back in Atlanta that he had met the woman he would marry.

In a love letter written during their courtship when they were temporarily apart, Doc wrote, "My life without you is like a year without springtime which comes to give illumination and heat to the atmosphere of winter.... Oh, excuse me, my darling. I didn't mean to go off on such a poetical and romantic flight. But how else can we express the deep emotions of life other than in poetry? Isn't love too ineffable to be grasped by the cold calculating hands of intellect?"

Coretta waited six months before accepting Doc's marriage proposal.

In June 1953, Daddy King officiated at the wedding ceremony; tellingly, Coretta insisted that the vows exclude all mention of the wife's obligation to "obey" her husband. Coretta had no interest in being a subservient wife.

When Doc's political activism kicked off in Montgomery in 1955, Coretta was by his side. She marched on the front lines. In 1957, she journeyed with him to Ghana to celebrate that nation's independence. In 1958, she joined him on a trip to India, where they paid homage to the legacy of Mahatma Gandhi. In 1962, she traveled alone to Geneva, Switzerland, where she was a delegate to the Women's Strike for Peace. In 1964, she participated in an early incarnation of the Women's Strike Force.

Since then Coretta has gone to mobilization rallies, where she is often asked to speak — not as Doc's surrogate but as a respected activist who uses a voice uniquely her own.

His ambivalence remains: while he values and loves her for who she is, he also wishes she could be a little more submissive. He has enough rebellious subordinates without having to count his wife among them.

Of all his subordinates, James Bevel is the most idiosyncratic — a man who, in the view of many, walks the thinnest of lines between brilliance and insanity. It is Bevel who suggests that many of the ministers attached to SCLC are burdened by the guilt of extramarital affairs. They need to confess their sins to their wives.

Doc's reaction is immediate: That's crazy. That's out of the question. That would accomplish nothing. Besides, many of Doc's spiritual-theology heroes have been sexually preoccupied. Saint Augustine. Martin Luther. The philosophers Søren Kierkegaard and Paul Tillich. Bevel rejects the argument. That was their problem. Our problem is to unburden our souls and be honest with our wives. Doc remains unmoved.

He thinks back to one of his earliest love affairs. It took place before he met Coretta, during his time at Crozer Theological Seminary in Pennsylvania. He was barely twenty-one. She was a white girl of German heritage. She was involved with a professor, but Doc quickly won over her heart. Their six-month romance was torrid. Doc fell head over heels in love. He spoke of marriage. His friends warned that such a union would prevent him from pastoring a church in the South, not to mention enrage his mom and dad. With great anguish and reluctance, he broke off the relationship.

Since his marriage to Coretta, Doc has been able to manage their emotional relationship, forming a tricky balance between love, devotion, responsibility, and guilt.

That delicate balance is upset, though, later in January 1968, when he learns that Coretta requires surgery for a stomach tumor. The thought of losing his wife fills him with fear. He cancels all engagements and remains by her side and in deep prayer. When the operation is successful and the tumor is seen as benign, he rejoices.

Then — quite remarkably and unexpectedly — Doc does the one thing he told James Bevel that he would never do: he confesses to Coretta that he has had an adulterous relationship. The confession is not comprehensive. But in Doc's mind the very fact of admitting infidelity is at least a move in the right direction. He will cut off this relationship. From now on, he promises his wife, he will walk the straight and narrow.

Having heard rumors of Doc's affairs, Coretta isn't shocked by his admission, but she is nonetheless hurt and angry. Even more furious is Juanita Abernathy, Ralph's wife, who cannot understand why Doc has chosen this delicate moment in Coretta's recovery to make his belated confession. Surely this is the wrong time and the wrong place.

The answer is simply that, in the aftermath of his wife's sudden surgery, guilt has overtaken him. Bevel had argued that confession is good for the soul. Doc's soul is in tremendous pain. To relieve that pain he needs to be honest with the wife whom he loves so dearly. To get himself right, he needs to get right with the mother of his children.

Spring is only a few months away, and after spending so much time and effort trying to sell his troops on the poverty campaign, and then so much time at home, Doc feels that there's no time to waste: he needs to give himself over to the upcoming poverty campaign in Washington.

And at the very moment when it seems that Doc's organization might finally be sold, the supporter for whom he has utmost respect restates his opposition to Doc's plan.

During several difficult seasons, Bayard Rustin argues that these upcoming protests in Washington will lead to "further backlash and repression." This is just what Doc does not want to hear. Doc desperately wants Bayard to back him. He needs the enthusiastic encouragement of a man respected as an exceptional strategist and deep thinker. If only Bayard could be on his side, Doc's political life at this point would be so much easier.

But Bayard, like Doc, is independent of mind. He is also a pragmatist convinced that his friend has lost his way. When it came to the great civil rights events that turned the tide of American history, their hearts and minds worked in harmony. It was a strong partnership: two towering intellectuals, two men instrumental in the formation of SCLC, two pacifist warriors risking their lives for the cause of equality. To lose Bayard's support leaves Doc that much more vulnerable — especially because so many other active participants in the movement have now joined the ranks of observers. They have moved to the sidelines to watch and critique.

Martin Luther King Jr., a man who has continually played offense, is now playing defense. Doc spends an inordinate amount of time defending himself against the sniping of critics, including former allies.

Among the most persistent critics is Adam Clayton Powell, who has ended his Bahamian exile and landed in California. Continuing his assault on Doc's creed of nonviolence, Powell tells the *New York Times* that the black revolution will soon become the "Second American Civil War."

Doc knows full well what Powell is doing: he is attempting to change with the changing times. Doc argues for the other path. He makes it clear that the job of the true believer—he who embraces the radical love ethos at the heart of Christianity—is not to change *with* the times but, through the force of his constant conviction, to change the times.

On February 1, Doc picks up the *Atlanta Journal-Constitution* and reads that the administration's military strategy in Vietnam has suffered a powerful blow. In what will soon be termed the Tet Offensive, the Vietcong and North Vietnamese have launched a series of surprise attacks. American and South Vietnamese forces are reeling. Tet is being called the largest operation in the history of this agonizingly long conflict, a stunning setback for Johnson and his hawks. Antiwar protestors are emboldened.

The very next day, the newspaper runs another item that catches Doc's eye, but this one is closer to home. It is a small story, but it greatly unsettles Doc's spirit.

In the midst of a thunderous rainstorm, two sanitation workers—Robert Walker, twenty-nine, and Echol Cole, thirty-five—were riding inside the compression unit of a garbage truck. According to city rules, there was only one place that black employees could seek shelter: in the storage cylinder containing the garbage. On this tragic day, the mechanism misfired and the men were crushed to death.

Doc is horrified.

He notes the dateline on the story:

Memphis, Tennessee.

*Chapter Fifteen*

# DRUM MAJOR

It is Sunday, February 4, and Memphis is on Doc's mind.

His prepared sermon, though, focuses on a psychological matter that has long intrigued him: the potential danger of unchecked ego. To the congregants of Ebenezer Baptist Church, he tells the story from the Gospel of St. Matthew of two brothers, James and John, who ask Jesus if they can sit beside him in glory.

After a short discussion, Jesus lays it on the line: "Whoever wants to become great among you must be your servant, and whoever wants to be first must be slave of all. For even the Son of Man did not come to be served, but to serve and give his life as a ransom for many."

Exploring the subject of self-celebration, Doc calls the request of James and John the "drum major instinct." He shows how the boastful man is a tiresome man, a morally distorted man. Doc shows how this instinct leads to "pushing others down in order to push yourself up." He relates it to racism—"a need that some people have to feel that they are first, and to feel that their white skin ordained them to be first." He relates it to exclusivism. "Not too long ago," he says, "a man down in Mississippi said that God was a charter member of the White Citizens Council. And so God being the charter member means that everybody who's in that has a kind of divinity, a kind of superiority. And think of what has happened in history as a result of this perverted use of the drum major instinct. It has led to the most tragic prejudice, the most tragic expressions of man's inhumanity to man."

In relating the psychological syndrome to racism, he offers deep compassion for those white folks afflicted by poverty.

"The drum major instinct [has you] thinking that you are somebody big because you are white. And you're so poor you can't send your children to school.... The poor white has been put into this position, where through blindness and prejudice, he is forced to support his oppressors. And the only thing he has going for him is the false feeling that he's superior because his skin is white—and can't hardly eat and make his ends meet week in and week out."

He applies his thesis to the notion of nationhood.

"This is why we are drifting. And we are drifting there because nations are caught up with the drum major instinct. 'I must be first.' 'I must be supreme.' 'Our nation must rule the world.' And I am sad to say that the nation in which we live is the supreme culprit.... God didn't call America to do what she's doing in the world now. God didn't call America to engage in a senseless, unjust war as the war in Vietnam.

And we are criminals in that war. We've committed more war crimes almost than any nation in the world...and we won't stop it because of our pride and our arrogance."

Then he brings it all back to Jesus. Jesus understands that James and John want to be great—and there's nothing wrong with greatness. But Jesus, the embodiment of radical love, alters the very meaning of greatness.

"Recognize that he who is greatest among you shall be your servant," Doc preaches. "That's a new definition of greatness.

"I know a man who was born in an obscure village...an itinerant preacher...didn't have much...never wrote a book... never held an office...never went to college...did none of the usual things that the world would associate with greatness...had no credentials but himself...was only thirty-three when the tide of public opinion turned against him....They called him a rabble-rouser...a troublemaker...an agitator... he practiced civil disobedience, he broke injunctions....His friends turned him over to his enemies, and while he was dying the people who killed him gambled for his clothing, the only possession that he had in the world....

"Nineteen centuries have come and gone and today he stands as the most influential figure that ever entered human history. All of the armies that ever marched, all the navies that ever sailed, all the parliaments that ever sat, and all the kings that ever reigned all put together have not affected the life of man on this earth as much as that one solitary life....He didn't have anything. He just went around serving and doing good."

Doc startles his congregants by shifting gears, moving from the narrative of Christ to chillingly prescient meditations on his own demise:

"Every now and then I think about my own death and I think about my own funeral. And I don't think of it in a morbid sense....I ask myself, 'What is it that I would want said?'...

"If any of you are around when I have to meet my day, I don't want a long funeral. And if you get somebody to deliver the eulogy, tell them not to talk too long. And every now and then I wonder what I want them to say. Tell them not to mention that I have a Nobel Peace Prize—that isn't important. Tell them not to mention that I have three or four hundred other awards—that's not important. Tell them not to mention where I went to school.

"I'd like somebody to mention that day that Martin Luther King, Jr., tried to give his life serving others.

"I'd like for somebody to say that day that Martin Luther King, Jr., tried to love somebody.

"I want you to be able to say that day that I tried to be right on the war question...say that I did try to feed the hungry...say that day that I did try in my life to clothe those who were naked...say that I was a drum major, say that I was a drum major for justice. Say that I was a drum major for peace. I was a drum major for righteousness. And all of the other shallow things will not matter. I won't have any money to leave behind. I won't have the fine and luxurious things of life to leave behind. But I just want to leave a committed life behind. And that's all I want to say."

*Chapter Sixteen*

---

# HUMILITY, LEVITY, AND LONGEVITY

The confrontation is nasty.

An assemblage of women that Doc presumed to be enthusiastic sympathizers verbally assaults him. The day after delivering his drum major sermon, Doc is back in the thick of it. He's in Chicago facing the outrage of representatives of the National Welfare Rights Organization.

He has come to the YMCA to share his grand vision of the Poor People's Campaign, which will descend on Washington in the spring. Latino migrant workers, Appalachian farmers, coal miners, ditchdiggers, and dishwashers — impoverished Americans of every color and religion — will march arm in arm to protest this nation's brutal economic inequality. They will encamp on the grounds of the Capitol and remain there until legislators heed their demands. Can

Doc count on the vast membership of the National Welfare Rights Organization to stand with him?

Hell no.

Not only are the women in no mood to hear about some high profile poverty demonstration, but they want to know what Doc knows about their agenda to reform the current welfare laws. They cross-examine him ruthlessly. Andy Young will later say that he has never seen Doc treated so insultingly.

"Do you know about Anti-Welfare Bill H.R. 12080, passed by Congress on December 15 and signed into law by Lyndon Baines Johnson on January 2?" asks one woman.

No, Doc answers honestly. He is not familiar with the bill.

"Where were you last October when we were down in Washington to get support for Senator Kennedy's amendments?"

Again Doc demurs, confessing that he is not conversant with those amendments. He admits ignorance and, rather than defend himself and his record — as his aides are quick to do — he invites the ladies to educate him about their legislative efforts. He knows that there will be no recruiting them for his campaign. His job is to simply sit and listen. He is humbled.

Then on a bright, sunny day he is marching in Washington, leading some twenty-five hundred members of the Clergy and Laymen Concerned about Vietnam on a vigil through Arlington National Cemetery. When he reaches the steps of the Tomb of the Unknown Soldier, Doc says simply,

"In this period of absolute silence, let us pray." For the next six minutes, eyes are closed, heads bowed.

Later, at the New York Avenue Presbyterian Church, a sanctuary, he is speaking, saying, "The war in Vietnam has exacerbated the tensions between the continents and between the races.... It does not help America and her so-called image to be the most powerful, richest nation in the world at war with one of the smallest poorest nations in the world that happens to be a colored nation."

He turns from guns to butter.

"When poor people and Negroes are way down in a depression situation economically, we call it a social ill, but when white people get massively unemployed we call it a depression. And the Negro is facing a depression.... When you get to the Negro youth, the unemployment is probably in some cities between 30% and 40%. Now this is a depression more staggering than the depression of the 30s."

Even as Doc continues to use the word "depression" to describe the plight of poor people, those in his inner circle apply that same word to his state of mind.

Looking back at this period, Andy Young will say, "He was given to a kind of depression that he had not had earlier. He talked about death all the time.... He couldn't relax, he couldn't sleep.... Even when we were away on trips, he'd want to talk all night long."

According to Coretta, "He got very depressed...a state of depression that was greater than I had ever seen before."

"I felt his weariness," Dorothy Cotton will remember. "The weariness of the whole struggle."

In the view of Clarence Jones, "he was never getting enough sleep, never able to eat regularly, torn by his obligations as a husband and father to his kids...constantly worrying about whether there was going to be enough money to meet payroll for SCLC."

"He was very unhappy," according to associate Gwendolyn Green. "He was depressed.... He was dark, gaunt and tired. He felt that his time was up.... He said that he knew that they were going to get him."

To the comedian Dick Gregory, Doc says the same thing. With tears in his eyes, Doc tells him he's certain that the end is near. He's certain that he'll be killed.

Yet no matter the depth of his despondency or fears, Doc stays on the front line, facing the threatening forces, both visible and invisible. Among the visible are those in the movement who continue to oppose his grand plans to dramatize the plight of the poor.

While still in Washington, he meets with Stokely Carmichael's Black United Front. At the gathering, one of SCLC's white members is denied entrance. The mood is sullen. The group not only questions Doc's spring poverty campaign but denigrates his celebrated Selma march by questioning his tactic of having turned around when confronted with the police barricade. Once again, Doc must play defense. Carmichael offers no support for Doc's poor people's project and calls it "a serious tactical error." He doesn't like its multiethnic hue. His only concession is not to oppose it.

The divide between Doc and Stokely — nonviolence versus violence — widens. Even as Doc's aides defend him against the militants' biting charges, Doc accuses his team of failing to defend nonviolence. His voice rises — he's angry and tired. He tells his people that his own prominence isn't important; what's important is the inviolable principle of nonviolence. He views some of his supporters as apologists. For an impassioned pacifist like Martin Luther King Jr., that's morally reprehensible.

Despite how dark and down he feels, Doc can't help being a humorist. In the midst of his insane travel schedule, the countless speeches and press conferences and board meetings and strategy sessions, Doc likes to cut up. He'll banter back and forth with the best of them. He'll come up with one-liners that can crack up the crowd. And though there is no doubt that, in the winter of 1968, he's experiencing increasing gloom and decreasing joviality, at times his mood can brighten.

On February 8, the day after the trying confrontation with the militants, he's downright funny. He's on national television in New York, where Harry Belafonte is substituting for Johnny Carson on *The Tonight Show*.

In the guest chair, Doc appears relaxed. Before getting serious, he describes his day thus far: "I flew out of Washington this afternoon, and as soon as we started out they notified us that the plane had mechanical difficulties.... Finally, we took off and landed, and whenever I land after mechanical difficulties I'm always very happy. Now, I don't want to give the impression that as a Baptist preacher I don't have faith in God in the air. It's simply that I've had more experience with Him on the ground."

Doc goes on to describe the harrowing trip from the airport to the television studio. Due to the late landing, he worried that he might miss the broadcast, and he urged the cabdriver to make haste. The cabbie's response was to drive so recklessly that Doc had to modify his original request and remind the man that he'd rather be "Dr. King who arrives late than the late Dr. King!"

For all the light banter, Belafonte does not avoid the troubling subject of Doc's vulnerability.

"Dr. King, do you ever fear for your life?" Belafonte asks.

"I'm far more concerned about doing something for humanity and what I consider the will of God than longevity. Ultimately it isn't so important how long you live. The important thing is how well you live."

Two days later, Doc is not well. He falls sick in Philadelphia, where he is due to speak, and is treated for an upper respiratory infection. When Walter P. Lomax Jr., a black physician, asks to take a photograph with him, Doc graciously agrees.

"Would you be good enough to write something for my children?" the physician asks.

Doc inscribes the words, "May you have a noble future."

Recovering from his illness, Doc still has Memphis

on his mind. Events in Memphis continue to demand his attention.

From his close friend and fellow activist-pacifist James Lawson, pastor of Centenary United Methodist Church in Memphis, Doc learns that, even in light of the recent tragedy, city officials have flat out refused to negotiate with the garbage workers. They will not consider pay increases or benefit improvements; they will not tolerate a union; they will not reexamine their safety regulations.

On February 11, Doc is back on his feet, back in Atlanta, and encouraged to learn that most of Memphis's sanitation workers—930 out of 1,100 men—have walked off the job. Lawson heads the strike committee. The mayor declares the strike illegal. No matter: the men are doing what needs to be done. Doc considers this an act of bold nonviolent protest. What alternative is there but to stop working and force the issue? The workers have no money, no power, no recognized union. Civil disobedience is their only weapon.

Memphis stays on Doc's mind.

The poverty encampment is also on his mind. He tells the SCLC Action Committee that "we are not doing our homework." He's concerned that without renewed effort the campaign will falter. Given the deep concern about the budgetary crisis, it's another difficult, drawn-out meeting.

If these truths don't seem to change, neither does the fact that Doc can't sit still for long, and in the middle of the month, the preacher is on the move again. At the break of dawn he's off to the airport. This time the mode of transportation has him concerned. It's a Cessna prop, a puddle jumper from Atlanta to Selma, Alabama, where he's due to speak. Beyond the fact that the plane is small, Doc worries that there's only one pilot. Without a backup, he's nervous. But he's also determined to recruit volunteers for the poverty campaign from among his core constituents doing civil rights work in the early sixties, and so he boards.

It's a bumpy landing and a quick drive to Tabernacle Baptist Church, where he tells those assembled that it was a treat to be met at the airport by a Negro deputy sheriff as opposed to the posse of Jim Clark, the white sheriff whose attitude about integration was expressed by the button he often wore: *"Never."*

Doc's speech focuses on poverty.

"What does it profit a man to be able to have access to any integrated lunch counter when he doesn't earn enough to take his wife out to dinner? What does it profit a man to have access to the motels of the highways and the hotels of the cities and not earn enough to take a vacation?"

Then it's back to the airport, back on the Cessna for a quick hop to Montgomery. Looking out the little window, Doc gazes down at Highway 80. His mind is flooded with memories. It was here on March 7, 1965, that Ralph Abernathy and Hosea Williams led protestors on a march from Selma. Their destination was the capitol in Montgomery. The issue was voting rights. The issue was also a recent murder. During a nonviolent protest a month earlier, Jimmie Lee Jackson, a twenty-six-year-old church deacon, was shot to death by a state trooper as Jackson shielded his mother from the trooper's nightstick.

The marchers were teargassed and brutalized. Young freedom rider John Lewis, his head bloodied from a billy club beating, looked into the television cameras and said, "I don't see how President Johnson can send troops to Vietnam, I don't see how he can send troops to the Congo, I don't see how he can send troops to Africa and can't send troops to Selma." Two days later, Doc ignored a court order and reinitiated the march, this time crossing the Edmund Pettus Bridge but turning back at the barricade of state troopers. On subsequent days, the marchers kept coming, finally reaching the Alabama state capitol. By then they were marching under the protection of the U.S. Army. Johnson had heeded Lewis's call. By August, the Voting Rights Act was the law of the land.

That was nearly three years ago. It was a moment when the movement won over the heart of a nation, a time when the startling effectiveness of peaceful protest was apparent to all. It was a victory to be cherished. Doc was lionized. He was satisfied that, despite the heartbreaking sacrifices made, his push for freedom for the disenfranchised had gained critical new ground.

As the Cessna makes its descent into Montgomery, Doc wonders if he can ever again make such dramatic strides. He wonders whether all the warring factions dividing his movement and the nation will ever coalesce.

"I've agonized over it," he tells the crowd that has come to hear him at Montgomery's Maggie Street Missionary

Baptist Church, "and I'm trying to save America. And that's what you're trying to do if you will join this movement."

He tells the gospel story of Dives, the rich man who goes to hell for not helping the beggar Lazarus. "Dives didn't go to hell because he was rich. Dives went to hell because he passed by Lazarus every day but never really saw him. Dives went to hell because he allowed Lazarus to become invisible. . . . If America doesn't use its vast resources and wealth to bridge the gap between the rich and poor nations, and between the rich and poor in this nation, it too is going to hell."

*America may be going to hell.*

Despite all the criticism swirling around him, despite all the push back that he endures, Doc continues to articulate the hard truths that he feels in his heart.

From Montgomery it's back on the Cessna and back to Atlanta, where Doc hopes to catch still another flight—to Detroit, where, that very evening, the city is celebrating Aretha Franklin Day with a gala concert.

As the Cessna bounces through the clouds, Doc entertains the questions of a reporter who has come along for the ride. Doc wants to promote his poverty campaign, but the reporter wants to discuss death—that is, previous assassination attempts. He wants to know about the most frightening moments in Doc's life.

Doc remembers a march in Philadelphia, Mississippi, last June, when he was told that the killers of Chaney, Goodman, and Schwerner—the three freedom riders—were there to kill him too. He also remembers the march in Chicago last August, at which he was pelted with rocks.

The interview hardly helps Doc's dark mood, but the thought of getting to Detroit does. He wants to honor the Queen of Soul, who has given so generously of her time to their cause. In Atlanta he quickly transfers from the Cessna to a commercial flight, arriving in Motor City just in time to dash over to Cobo Hall and take the stage, where he presents Aretha with a special award from SCLC. The Queen is thrilled at Doc's surprise appearance, and Doc is thrilled to kick back and hear her tear up "(You Make Me Feel Like) A Natural Woman."

Doc feels the song deep in his soul. Aretha is singing the blues. She's singing about getting up, looking out on a gloomy day, and feeling "so uninspired." She's singing about having to face another day, and she's moaning, "Lord, it made me feel so tired."

Doc's had a long, long day.

Atlanta.

Selma.

Montgomery.

Back to Atlanta.

Up to Detroit, where Aretha is singing about the time her soul was in the lost and found.

Doc relates.

He's been lost.

He's been found.

He's still searching. Still moving, always moving.

Tomorrow he'll rush back to Atlanta.

Sunday he'll preach.

Sunday night he's off again—this time to a big ministers' meeting in Miami.

The drive never diminishes.

The travel never stops.

Bone weary, on the edge of nervous exhaustion, downhearted and far from home, Doc is nonetheless grateful to be in Detroit. The music calms his spirit. The music refreshes his soul.

Aretha is singing, "You make me feel so alive."

Doc is feeling that, despite it all, these are the small miraculous moments that push him to keep on keeping on.

## Chapter Seventeen

# FRANTIC MELANCHOLY

If Doc is able to deal with the darkness — a darkness whose history includes thoughts of suicide and a preoccupation with death — it is because of his unstoppable drive to attend to the least among us. There is, though, this precarious balance between his ups and his downs. He is torn between bleakness and light, despair and hope. Taylor Branch would later describe Doc's emotional condition in these, his final days, as one of "frantic melancholy."

On February 18, he is back home in the pulpit of Ebenezer delivering a sermon that he calls "Who Is My Neighbor?" In it he tells Jesus's story of the Good Samaritan: A man has been beaten and left for dead on the side of a road. A priest and another cleric see him, ignore him, and move on. It is the outsider, the nonecclesiastical Good Samaritan, who saves the man's life.

In an act of public confession, Doc surprises his congregation. Rather than identifying with the Good Samaritan, he sees himself as the heartless priest. Doc speaks of the time that he bypassed a hitchhiker on a desolate highway outside Atlanta.

"I really haven't gotten over it to this day," he says. "I didn't stop to help the man because I was afraid."

Fear returns when, on the Monday after his Sunday sermon, he is in Miami to give the opening speech at a leadership conference of one hundred and fifty Negro pastors and learns of threats to his life.

Ignoring the threats, he addresses the convocation, his words reflecting his own personal struggle:

"When hope diminishes, the hate element is often turned toward those who originally built up the hope. The bitterness is often greater toward that person who built up the hope, who could say 'I have a dream,' but couldn't produce the dream because of the failure and the sickness of the nation to respond to the dream."

There can be no doubt that he is referring to himself.

There can also be no doubt that the death threats are real. The FBI has received a bomb threat. A man identifying himself as a sniper with every intention of murdering the minster has called the Sheraton hotel, where Doc is staying, and demanded to know his room number. The Miami police insist that Doc remain secluded for the rest of the five-day conference. Armed security officers are stationed in front of his room.

Billy Kyles, a well-known minister from Memphis, is in the room with Doc, whose nerves are frayed. Obsessed with dark memories, Doc once again recounts those other times when his life was on the line — the frightening marches in Mississippi, experiencing the murderous hatred of the rock throwers in Cicero, Illinois.

Murderous hatred is rampant in Memphis. Reverend Kyles learns that, while he and Doc are holed up in this hotel room, demonstrators have been maced. Kyles's daughter is among the injured marchers protesting on behalf of the sanitation workers.

Memphis is on the verge of mayhem.

The calls between Memphis and Miami heat up. Doc and Kyles's mutual friend Reverend James Lawson reports from the front line. He is alarmed that the press is giving the strikers scant notice. Lawson sees this as a national issue and is convinced that national leaders — like Doc — must come to Memphis to direct media focus on the mounting crisis.

Doc is moved but also reluctant. His Poor People's Campaign is still unformed and in desperate need of all his attention. Beyond that, the police and the FBI are warning him to curtail his movement in public.

For four days Doc is mostly restricted to his room. From a distance of mere yards that feel like miles, he learns that the conference is chaotic. The militants will not yield to the more moderate ministers and accuse them of selling out. It's another exercise in hostility—and this among clergymen who supposedly espouse teachings of tolerance and love.

It is the ethos of love that Doc espouses when, unable to remain in his room any longer, he emerges to address the conference during its last day.

"We didn't come to Miami to play," he tells his fellow preachers. "We came to Miami to see how we could develop a relevant and a creative ministry for the valley." He speaks of a valley filled with "men and women who know the ache and anguish of poverty.... Welfare mothers who'll not be able to feed their little children.... People who are in moments of despair because of their circumstances."

Doc rises above his own circumstances as a marked man. In a plea for unity among the ministers, he asserts, "We will influence the policies of every city if we in this room will just stick together, and work together, and love each other."

Although it is with love, he goes on to deliver a sharp moral assessment of many of his fellow preachers.

"Let us admit that even the black church has often been a tail-light rather than a headlight." He admonishes the clergymen for not confronting the great sociopolitical issues of our time. Even as congregants live "in the midst of... poverty," he cannot abide ministers who preach "pious irrelevancies and sanctimonious trivialities." He rebukes his colleagues for their obsession with rampant materialism. "Too often we've been more concerned about the size of the wheelbase on our automobiles, and the amount of money we get on our anniversaries." His call is to "give a kind of new vitality to the religion of Jesus Christ." He believes that "the great tragedy is that Christianity failed to see that it had the revolutionary edge."

His speech over, Doc is rushed from the conference to the airport to fly to New York, where some five hours later— on the evening of February 23—he appears on the stage of Carnegie Hall to honor one of his revolutionary heroes, W. E. B. Du Bois, the intellectual giant who cofounded the NAACP.

Although Doc strikes many in the audience, including his friend Stanley Levison, as tired and out of sorts, he nonetheless uses the occasion to reassert his belief in radical solutions to social ills.

"We cannot talk of Dr. Du Bois," he says, "without recognizing that he was a radical all of his life."

Doc contrasts Du Bois's militancy with the militancy currently in vogue:

"He [Du Bois] confronted the establishment as a model of militant manhood and integrity. He defied them and though they heaped venom and scorn on him his powerful voice was never stilled.

"And yet, with all his pride and spirit he did not make a mystique out of blackness. He was proud of his people, not because their color endowed them with some vague greatness but because their concrete achievements in struggle had advanced humanity and he saw and loved progressive humanity in all its hues, black, white, yellow, red and brown.

"Above all he did not content himself with hurling

invectives for emotional release and then to retire into smug passive satisfaction. History had taught him it is not enough for people to be angry—the supreme task is to organize and unite people so that their anger becomes a transforming force....

"This life style of Dr. Du Bois is the most important quality this generation of Negroes needs to emulate. The educated Negro who is not really part of us and the angry militant who fails to organize us have nothing in common with Dr. Du Bois. He exemplified Black power in achievement and he organized Black power in action. It was no abstract slogan to him."

With the speech behind him, Doc still fears that the militant Black Power sloganeers have captured the imagination of the youth. Photographed wearing dark glasses and with a rifle in hand, Stokely Carmichael has been declared "Prime Minister of the Black Nation" in an attempt to unite the Black Panther Party and SNCC. "Black nationalism," he declares, "must be our ideology." In truth, there is mounting dissent on the left. "The SNCC people were the bad niggers in town, and then the Panthers jumped up and started saying, 'We are badding you out,'" says SNCC leader Willie Ricks. The fact that Doc's opponents are disorganized brings him no comfort. He is deeply disturbed by any disunity among black folks, even his adversaries.

Reverberating are lines of a poem by William Butler Yeats, written nearly a half century earlier in response to Europe's moral collapse in the wake of World War I.

*Things fall apart; the center cannot hold;*
*Mere anarchy is loosed upon the world,*
*The blood-dimmed tide is loosed, and everywhere*
*The ceremony of innocence is drowned;*
*The best lack all conviction, while the worst*
*Are full of passionate intensity.*

Doc has conviction, but the intensity of these past weeks—these past months, this past year—has Doc on the verge of physical and mental collapse. Rather than risk a complete breakdown, he agrees to a short vacation in Jamaica with Coretta. Aide Andy Young comes along.

The vacation is marred by distractions. "The tourists wouldn't leave us alone and the phone was our enemy," Doc later tells Stanley Levison.

Even more disturbing are the news accounts of Bayard Rustin's pointed criticisms of Doc's Poor People's Campaign. Rather than restrict the airing of his dissent to members of SCLC, Rustin goes to the press and says, "I seriously question the efficacy of Dr. King's plans for the April project." He believes that the protest would not favorably influence Congress. The way forward, according to Rustin, is by electing Democratic candidates who favor progressive legislation, not mass demonstrations. He urges Doc to cancel his plans, and even if Doc might lose face, "he'll lose a lot more face if he conducts the demonstrations and fails."

The growing estrangement between Doc and Rustin,

once the closest of colleagues and political-spiritual soul mates, is a source of profound pain for Doc.

Doc's pain is evident when, back from a restless vacation and addressing his congregation at Ebenezer, his Sunday sermon focuses on unfulfilled dreams. Doc's mood remains downcast.

He describes how King David never lived to see his dream of a temple in Jerusalem. Gandhi never lived to see his dream of a free India. Paul never lived to see his dream of reaching Spain. Most folks don't live to see their dreams of a better world or a fulfillment of their own better character.

"You don't need to go out this morning saying that Martin Luther King is a saint. Oh no," he exclaims, "I want you to know this morning that I'm a sinner like all of God's children."

He seeks the comfort that God offered David. While David's dream was not fulfilled, the Lord did tell David that, in Doc's interpretation, "it is well that it is within thine heart. It's well that you are trying. You may not see it. The dream may not be fulfilled, but...thank God this morning that we do have hearts to put something meaningful in."

President Johnson's dream of a quick end to the war in Vietnam continues to exist only in fantasy. Despite massive bombings, the administration's war strategy is proving untenable. With more than a half-million troops already engaged, the military command is requesting two hundred thousand more. The president is caught up in a spiral of frustration.

The spiral intensifies when, on March 1, the president's National Advisory Commission on Civil Disorders, known as the Kerner Commission, issues its public report. The findings on the causes of the 1967 urban riots are unequivocal: "White racism is essentially responsible for the explosive mixture which has been accumulating in our cities since the end of World War II." The report's most widely quoted statement could not be clearer: "Our nation is moving toward two societies, one black, one white — separate and unequal."

Mired in the confusion of his war policy — it is costing three times the amount of money that the president's own commission is urging the government to invest in our cities — LBJ does not comment on the Kerner report.

Doc does.

"The Commission's finding that America is a racist society and that white racism is the root cause of today's urban disorders is an important confession of a harsh truth," he tells the press before relating the conclusions to poverty. According to Doc, all this shows how "the lives, the incomes, the well-being of poor people everywhere in America are plundered by our economic system." He stresses "the absolute necessity of our spring campaign in Washington." Doc goes on to describe how three separate caravans — from Mississippi, Milwaukee, and Massachusetts — will descend on the Capitol. He envisions folks arriving by the hundreds of thousands — by car and truck, by foot and even mule cart. He sees this poor people's march transforming the very consciousness of the nation.

Reporters want to know when it will happen.

In late April, early May.

That's only eight weeks away.

Can Doc pull this off?

He assures the questioners that he can.

At the same time, he does not reveal how his plans are still under attack from within the very organization that he leads. In private, he is in a heated debate with Marian Logan, the wife of his friend and physician, Arthur Logan. Marian, in solidarity with Bayard Rustin, has written her fellow SCLC board members an impassioned argument against Doc's campaign:

"The demonstrations may well harden congressional resistance and create an atmosphere conducive not only to the victory of reactionary candidates in the coming elections, but also to the defeat of those candidates who are, or would be friendly to the social and economic objectives of our struggle."

She also writes directly to Doc, saying that he may not "be able to preserve the non-violent image and integrity of our organization.... You say, Martin, that you 'will use disruptive tactics only as a last resort'...but you understand, of course, that in view of the likely police response to these disruptive tactics, you are in effect saying that you are prepared to court violence as a last resort." She goes on to question the adequacy of the planning itself that, in her view, remains in a precarious state of disarray.

Doc's hope is that another short escape — this time to Acapulco — might repair his own state of disarray. But the melancholy does not lift. In the middle of the night, Ralph Abernathy, who has traveled with Doc, spots him on the balcony of his hotel room, where he is leaning over the rail. Abernathy is alarmed. He remembers Doc's story about a suicide attempt in his youth. He rushes to Doc's side.

"Martin," he says, "what are you doing out here this time of night? What's troubling you?"

After several moments of silence, Doc says, "You see that rock out there?"

"Yes, I see it."

"How long do you think it's been there?"

"I really don't know. Centuries and centuries."

"Do you know what I'm thinking about?"

Abernathy is reluctant to answer.

Mournfully, Doc begins to sing the ancient hymn "Rock of Ages," a meditation on eternal rest.

On the way home, Doc runs into Reverend Billy Graham at the airport. In the fifties, Graham had invited Doc to preach at a revival and subsequently contributed money to his cause. There is great mutual respect between the two Baptist preachers. This time, though, Graham is not reassuring. He is convinced that Doc is moving too aggressively with his social action programs — and cautions him to slow down.

Instead, Doc picks up the pace. He enthusiastically tells

an audience at New York's Hunter College about the upcoming Poor People's Campaign. The media is talking about "the long hot summer ahead," he says. "And what always bothers me about this is that the long hot summer has been preceded by a long cold winter. And the tragedy is that the nation has failed to use its winters creatively, compassionately.... And our nation's summers of riots are still caused by our nation's winters of delay."

Without delay, he sends a telegram to United Farm Workers leader Cesar Chavez saying that he is behind his twenty-five-day fast in support of striking farmworkers:

"I am deeply moved by your courage in fasting as your personal sacrifice for justice through nonviolence.... The plight of your people and ours is so grave that we all desperately need the inspiring example and effective leadership you have given."

Meanwhile, Memphis won't go away.

Memphis's black leadership is pressuring Doc to come to the city as the situation worsens with every passing day. The garbage strikers are gaining no ground. The powers that be continue to refuse their demands. Reverend James Lawson wants Doc to address the grievances and lend his great prestige to their noble cause.

Doc is torn.

The Poor People's Campaign requires all his attention, but Memphis is calling. Memphis stays on his mind.

In the midnight hour, unable to sleep in still another hotel room in still another city, Doc finds himself singing those same words he sang in Acapulco. It is the ancient hymn whose meaning penetrates his heart.

*Nothing in my hand I bring*
*Simply to Thy cross I cling*
*Naked, come to Thee for dress*
*Helpless, look to Thee for grace*
*Foul, I to the fountain fly*
*Wash me, Saviour, or I die*

*While I draw this fleeting breath*
*When mine eyes shall close in death*
*When I soar to worlds unknown*
*See Thee on Thy judgment throne*
*Rock of Ages, cleft for me*
*Let me hide myself in Thee*

*Chapter Eighteen*

# RESTLESS HEART

As a devoted student of theology, Doc is versed in the seminal texts of Christianity. Among those is *The Confessions of Saint Augustine,* the radically introspective fourth century autobiography that glorifies God even as it questions God's unknowable ways:

"Man is one of your creatures, Lord, and his instinct is to praise you. He bears about him the mark of death, the sign of his own sin, to remind him that you thwart the proud. But still, since he is a part of your creation, he wishes to praise you. The thought of you stirs him so deeply that he cannot be content unless he praises you, because you have made us for yourself and our hearts find no peace until they rest in you."

Then: "My soul is like a house, small for you to enter, but I pray you to enlarge it. It is in ruins, I ask you to remake it."

Augustine says that the human heart is restless until it reposes in God.

Doc's friends note that he is more restless than ever. Haunted by thoughts of ruination—the destruction of his own life, the destruction of his plans to help the poor—he reacts by moving at an even more frantic pace.

In Atlanta, he attends a summit meeting of seventy-eight "nonblack" minority leaders, including representatives from various Native American tribes, Chicanos, Puerto Ricans, and Appalachian whites. Like every other conference in the past year, it proves contentious and inconclusive. Embittered criticism from Doc's own SCLC staff remains unrelenting.

"Now he's taking our money and giving it to the Indians," says Hosea Williams.

From there, Doc rushes to catch a flight to Detroit, where that night he will deliver a major address in the wealthy suburb of Grosse Pointe before the town's Human Relations Council and a largely white audience. Nearly three thousand people eagerly await Doc's arrival. Also waiting is an angry throng of screaming protestors with signs that say "Traitor!" and "Commie!" On the final leg of the car trip from downtown Detroit to Grosse Pointe, the chief of police, concerned about a rash of ominous threats, bodily protects Doc by actually sitting on his lap.

The minute Doc arrives, the jeering picks up. Despite the presence of a riot squad, security guards are unable to keep the dissidents from entering the hall, where they get even louder, heckling Doc throughout his address. Rather than speak over them, Doc pauses and politely allows them to voice their views before returning to his remarks. Getting through his text is a struggle.

"I've been in the struggle a long time now," Doc tells the audience, "and I've conditioned myself to some things that are much more painful than discourteous people not allowing you to speak, so if they feel that they can discourage me, they'll be up here all night."

At one point he invites a particularly boisterous heckler, who has accused Doc of treason, to the stage. The man is a navy veteran who says, "I fought for freedom, not for communism...and I didn't fight to be sold down the drain."

Doc listens courteously. His measured response is simple: "We love our boys who are fighting there and we just want them to come back home."

For now, this heckler is stilled. But the others are not. The nasty insults keep coming.

In spite of the continual interruptions, Doc articulates his argument for his Poor People's Campaign — in his view, the only way to avert riots this coming summer — before addressing his tormentors head-on:

"In the midst of the hollering and in the midst of the discourtesy tonight, we see that, however much we dislike it, the destinies of white and black America are tied together....We must all learn to live together as brothers in this country or we're all going to perish together as fools....Every white person is a little bit Negro and every Negro is a little bit white. Our language, our music, our material prosperity, and even our food are an amalgam of black and white. So there can be no separate black path to power and fulfillment that does not intersect white routes. And there can be no separate white path to power and fulfillment short of social disaster without recognizing the necessity of sharing that power with black aspirations for freedom and human dignity. We do need each other: The black man needs the white man to save him from his fear and the white man needs the black man to free him from his guilt."

Raising his voice above the intransigent hecklers, Doc invokes the movement's signature song:

"We shall overcome because Thomas Carlyle is right. 'No lie can live forever.' We shall overcome because William Cullen Bryant is right. 'Truth crushed to earth will rise again.' We shall overcome because James Russell Lowell is right. 'Truth forever on the scaffold, wrong forever on the throne. Yet that scaffold sways the future, and behind the dim unknown standeth God in the shadows, keeping watch above his own'.... We shall overcome because the Bible is right. 'You shall reap what you sow.'"

The speech concluded, Doc is relieved to have outlasted the dissidents. In the aftermath of so much ugly contention, he says at a press conference that he has never before faced an indoor audience this hostile.

Only later does he learn that Rosa Parks, now employed by Michigan congressman John Conyers, was in the audience that night too.

Doc would have loved to have greeted his old friend and fellow soldier—to reminisce about those times, an eon ago, when they met back in Montgomery. So much has changed. So much has not changed. So many victories celebrated. So many defeats suffered. So many obstacles still in place. So much still to be done.


Doc's next stop is California. Another long flight over the Rockies into Los Angeles, and then he will be driven down to Anaheim to speak at the Disneyland Hotel, only to return the next day to preach a sermon in South Central Los Angeles.

Before he arrives at the "happiest place on earth," he receives advance notice that Bobby Kennedy will be announcing his candidacy for president and opposing Eugene McCarthy as they both seek to stop LBJ's renomination at the Democratic convention in Chicago, five months from now, in August.

Knowing that Doc will never support Johnson, Kennedy's people request that he withhold any endorsement of McCarthy and, short of declaring for Bobby, at least remain neutral. Doc agrees. For the moment, he's encouraged by the fact that the powerful Kennedys are prepared to take on a president whose war policies he so deeply abhors.

Discouragement, though, permeates the tone of his remarks in Anaheim.

"A riot is the language of the unheard," he says. "What is it that America has failed to hear? It has failed to hear that the plight of the poor has worsened over the last few years. It has failed to hear that promises of freedom and democracy have not been met. It has failed to hear that large segments of white society are more concerned about tranquility and the status quo than about justice and humanity."

While in Los Angeles, Doc has dinner with former Dodger pitcher Don Newcombe, one of the first Negroes — after Jackie Robinson and Roy Campanella — to integrate the big leagues in the late forties.

Newcombe is alarmed that Doc looks so haggard. His voice is strained and his eyes are filled with fatigue.

"You need some rest, Doc," says Newk.

Doc explains that his schedule won't allow it. "My brothers and sisters need me," he tells the pitcher before adding, "Don, you'll never know how easy you and Jackie and Campy made it for me to do my job by what you did on the baseball field."

The comment startles Newk.

"Doc," he says, "you're the one who got beat by billy clubs and bitten by dogs and thrown in jail. And you say we made *your* job easier — I don't get it."

"You were there first," says Doc. "I just followed."


An overflowing crowd follows Doc's every word.

It's Sunday morning and he's preaching at L.A.'s Holman United Methodist Church, declaring, "It is midnight in race relations in our country....Clouds of despair are floating in so many of our mental skies."

As in virtually all Doc's sermons, the emotional movement is from darkness to light; he works to turn the corner from despair to hope. Yet negotiating that turn is increasingly difficult. To realize that turn on this Sunday morning, he contrasts hope with desire.

"Hope is not desire.... You may desire money, but you hope for peace. You may desire sex, but you hope for freedom. You may desire beautiful clothes, but you hope for the ringing of justice. You see, desire has an 'I' quality, but hope has a 'we' quality.... I've seen people who have lost hope. They wander through life, but somehow they never live life.... They merely exist.... I have seen hate, and all the time I see it, I say to myself, 'Hate is too great a burden to bear.' I don't want to be like that.... It is only through love that we keep hope alive.... Hope is based on faith that life has ultimate meaning."

Doc has preached himself into a state of hope. For now the dark clouds have passed and he can look forward to flying to Atlanta. But then comes the call.

Memphis is calling.

Reverend James Lawson is on the line again. Lawson is a man whose integrity Doc cannot doubt. Lawson's argument carries mighty moral weight. Lawson is telling Doc that the strike in Memphis is a strike at the very heart of all that is wrong with America. The strike is now in its fifth full week. The strike has pitted the haves against the have-nots. The strike has expanded: a boycott of downtown stores has driven down retail sales 35 percent. But the strike needs further backing. Memphis is a microcosm of the great sociopolitical maladies plaguing the country. Memphis merits attention. Memphis merits support. Memphis is the nexus. Memphis requires, deserves, even demands the presence of Martin Luther King Jr.

Doc wants to fly back to Atlanta.

Wants to get back to Coretta and the kids.

Wants to resolve the bickering within SCLC.

Wants to pour all his energy into his Poor People's Campaign.

But how can he ignore Reverend Lawson's pleas?

How can he ignore Memphis's urgent call?

He wants to go home, he wants to stay on schedule, but how can he avoid Memphis when Memphis stays locked in his mind?

Memphis won't leave him alone.

Yes, he tells Lawson. He'll come to Memphis.

He'll be there tomorrow.

## Chapter Nineteen

# GARMENT OF DESTINY

*Listen, people, listen*
*I'm gonna sing you a song*
*About a man who lived good*
*But didn't live too long*

*He was born in Macon, Georgia*
*A poor boy without a dime*
*He found his way to Memphis*
*Singing "These Arms of Mine"*

The radio is tuned to WDIA, the "mother station of Negroes," the "heart and soul of Memphis," where William Bell is singing the tribute that he and organist Booker T. Jones have written in memory of Otis Redding, killed in a plane crash only three months earlier. The loss of Otis — the most luminous star to emerge from Memphis's own

Stax Records — at age twenty-six is especially painful. His last recording, the mournful "(Sittin' on) The Dock of the Bay," is in heavy rotation.

Memphis is in heavy mourning. The deep soul of Memphis is aching. The city that sits on the banks of the muddy Mississippi and calls itself the "gateway to the Delta" is torn asunder in a monumental clash between the powerful and the powerless. The usual sweet fragrance of barbecue is replaced with the stink of refuse.

Doc hears Memphis's music. He feels Memphis's pain. He knows this city's hallowed history and has accepted the fact that the passion and purpose of his own mission have made his journey here inevitable.

On Monday, March 18, as he is driven to Memphis's Mason Temple to rally the garbage strikers and their supporters, he gathers his strength. When he arrives at the huge hall, he is told that there is not, as expected, a crowd of ten thousand. The news disappoints him. "No," says an aide, "there are more than *15,000* supporters waiting to hear you." Doc is heartened. They're standing in the aisles, cheering and waving.

The reception is thunderous. Compared with the contempt that he has endured at the hands of right-wingers in Michigan and left-wing militants on both coasts, here he is celebrated as a conquering hero. But he quickly turns the attention from himself to the striking workers:

"You are demonstrating that we are all tied in a single garment of destiny."

He is also quick to humble himself. Referring to his

alma mater, he says, "The man who has been to 'No House' is as significant as the man who's been to Morehouse.... The person who picks up our garbage is as significant as the physician....All labor has worth.... You are reminding not only Memphis but the nation that it is a crime for people to live in this rich nation and receive starvation wages.... The vast majority of Negroes in our country are still perishing on a lonely island of poverty in a vast ocean of material prosperity....

"I will hear America through her historians years and years to come saying, 'We built gigantic buildings to kiss the sky. We built gargantuan bridges to span the sea. Through our spaceships we were able to carve highways through the stratosphere. Through our airplanes we were able to dwarf distances and place time in chains. Through our submarines we were able to penetrate oceanic depths.' But it seems that I can hear the God of the universe saying, 'Even though you've done all of that, I was hungry and you fed me not. I was naked and you clothed me not.' "

Doc repeats his prophetic warning that has become something of a mantra:

*America may be going to hell.*

Reaffirming the strikers, he says, "You have assembled for more than thirty days now to say, 'We are tired of being at the bottom. We are tired of being trampled over by the iron feet of oppression. We are tired of having our children attend overcrowded, inferior schools. We are tired of having to live in dilapidated, sub-standard housing conditions... where we don't have wall-to-wall carpet but so often end up with wall-to-wall rats and roaches. We are tired of smothering in an air-tight cage of poverty...tired of walking the streets for jobs that do not exist...tired of our men being emasculated so that our wives and our daughters have to go out and work in the white ladies' kitchens'....

"So in Memphis we have begun. We are saying, 'Now is the time.' Get the word out to everybody in power in this town that now is the time....

"Never forget that freedom is not something that is voluntarily given by the oppressor. It is something that must be demanded by the oppressed. Freedom is not some lavish dish that the power structure...will hand down on a silver platter while the Negro merely furnishes the appetite. If we are going to get equality, if we are going to get adequate wages, we are going to have to struggle for it....

"You may have to escalate the struggle....If they keep refusing and will not recognize the union...I'm telling you what you are going to have to do....You ought to get together and just have a general work stoppage in the city of Memphis. If you let that day come, not a Negro in this city will go to any job downtown. And not a Negro in domestic service will go to anybody's house or anybody's kitchen. And black students and teachers will not go to anybody's school. And they will hear you then. The city of Memphis will not be able to function."

His mind moves from Memphis to Washington. He sets out his grand vision to occupy the nation's capital for weeks on end.

"I ask you to make this the beginning of the Washington movement—We are going to start moving out.... We're going to have mule trains moving on up.... We're going to pick up forces in Alabama.... Those forces will join with Georgia.... Another group come on out of Milwaukee, Chicago...coming out of Pittsburgh...coming on down from Boston, New York, Philadelphia, Baltimore...moving on into Washington....

"Some of the Congressmen will stand at the windows of Congress. They will turn around and say, 'Who are these people? Where are they coming from?'...I want someone to say, 'These are they who are tired of years of oppression and denial.... These are they who are coming up out of great trials and tribulation'....

"We aren't going to Washington for one day this time. We're going to stay.... We're going to get flatbed trucks and take some shacks on those trucks.... We're going to take a shack by the Smithsonian Institute so that it can stand as a symbol of American life.... We're going to build a shanty town in Washington.... We're going to call it our 'City of Hope'.... Sunday after Sunday we're going to march around the walls of Capitol Hill. And we're going to keep on marching until the walls of injustice come tumbling down."

On its feet, the crowd goes wild. Doc has caught the spirit of Memphis and lifted it to new heights. As he leaves the podium, his aides hand him a note. He smiles and returns to the lectern.

"I want to tell you that I am coming back to Memphis on Friday to lead you in a march through the center of the city."

The shouting gets louder; the clamor is deafening. It feels as though the roof is coming off.

Doc is whisked away to the black-owned Lorraine Motel in the shadow of downtown, a favorite spot for celebrities like Ray Charles and Count Basie. The Lorraine is known as one of the few places in the city where blacks and whites can comfortably socialize. Memphis ministers Billy Kyles and Benjamin Hooks are with Doc, reviewing his triumphant address and planning what is certain to be his triumphant return at week's end. In a fitting conclusion to a remarkable evening, a choir of college women, also staying at the Lorraine, serenades Doc with songs of holy praise.

The sweet sound of their voices relaxes his soul. It is with both gratitude and resignation that, slipping into sleep, he accepts one inescapable truth:

His fate is tied to the fortune of this city's impoverished citizens, this city of Memphis.

Tuesday morning. The preacher is up, out, and moving on. It's puddle-hopping time again. A little Cessna will fly him deeper down the Delta, where Doc has scheduled no fewer than eight recruiting rallies over two days in rural Mississippi towns. There's not a minute to waste.

The first stop is at a broken-down church in Marks, Mississippi, located in the poorest county in America.

Despite the intrusion of an inebriated white man, Doc is moved to tears by the testimonies of women — one who says that her family barely subsists on a diet of pinto beans, another who cannot send her kids to school because they lack sufficient clothing.

Marks, Doc decides, is where the Poor People's mule train to Washington will commence.

From Marks to Clarksdale to Greenwood, where he is still haunted by the women of Marks:

"I wept with them as I heard them talking about the fact that they didn't even have any blankets to cover their children up on a cold night. I said to myself, 'God doesn't like this.' And we are going to say in no uncertain terms that we aren't going to accept it any longer. We've got to go to Washington in big numbers....We're going to make this nation move again, and we're going to make America see poor people."

From the poor of Greenwood and on to the poor of Grenada and Laurel and Hattiesburg and Jackson, where, due to the long rallies along the way, Doc arrives four hours late. The volunteers to join his effort are few, but he keeps on preaching.

He tells the crowd in Jackson that after giving his speech in Memphis and many more, "I [have] just about lost my voice. But we're going from here to tour Alabama and then on to Georgia and then we're going to move right on through the nation to outline this program." When his voice finally fades, he turns to Ralph Abernathy to do the actual recruiting.

By Wednesday his voice is barely back. But he presses on.

"Many of you are unemployed," he tells the gathering in Eutaw, Alabama. "You don't have adequate jobs, you don't have anything to lose. But by going to Washington, you have everything to gain."

Once again he paints a picture of a shantytown up on the great Mall, only this time, as part of the protest encampment, he expands his vision to include festivals of music, art, poetry, and science.

"We're going to let them know that Shakespeare was not the only poet that entered history, but Countee Cullen and Langston Hughes came by. We're going to let them know that Einstein wasn't the only scientist, but that George Washington Carver came by. Every day we're going to learn a little more about our heritage.... We're going to have a mighty time in Washington."

Like the good Baptist preacher that he is, Doc wraps up with an altar call:

"All ye who are burdened down, come unto us. All ye who are heavy laden, come unto us. All ye who are unemployed, come unto us. All ye who are tired of segregation and discrimination, come unto us. All ye who are overworked and underpaid, come unto us.... Put on your walking shoes and walk together, pray together, struggle together, believe together, have faith together, and come on to Washington. And there will be a great camp meeting in the Promised Land!"

It's a triumphant note, but bad weather dampens the momentum, cancels the remainder of his Alabama rallies.

Then bad news of the tepid response to Doc's recruitment drive is personally brought to President Johnson by J. Edgar Hoover. The spies inside SCLC have told the FBI that, for all Doc's efforts in the Delta, only a thousand dollars has been raised. Prospects for Doc's dream of a spectacular monthlong mass demonstration are growing dim.

But then there is Friday, and there is Memphis.

Memphis is the rallying point, the new hope of a movement that many see as dissipating and close to dissolution. Memphis will turn it around. Memphis will be the scene of Friday's triumphant march. In Memphis supporters will rally in great numbers. Memphis will renew the energy for positive change and put Doc's campaign back on track.

But strangely enough, here in the third week of March, an unseasonable blizzard is blasting its way through the Delta. A blanket of fresh snow has covered Memphis, and before Doc leaves for the airport, James Lawson calls to say that the march has been postponed.

A lover of literature, Doc is well aware of the concept of pathetic fallacy — when writers imbue nature with human emotions.

He can't help but see the snow as carrying a weight of sadness.

Only weeks earlier, citing the poet Henry Wadsworth Longfellow to those questioning his pacifism, Doc said, "May it not be that the new man the world needs is the nonviolent man? Longfellow said, 'In this world a man must either be an anvil or a hammer.' We must be hammers shaping a new society rather than anvils molded by the old."

That was the upbeat Longfellow. But there was also the downbeat Longfellow, who wrote something else:

*Silent, and soft, and slow*
*Descends the snow.*
*Even as our cloudy fancies take*
*Suddenly shape in some divine expression,*
*Even as the troubled heart doth make*
*In the white countenance confession,*
*The troubled sky reveals*
*The grief it feels.*
*This is the poem of the air,*
*Slowly in silent syllables recorded;*
*This is the secret of despair.*

*Chapter Twenty*

# FIREMEN

It is Saturday, March 23, and Doc introduces his two young sons, Martin III and Dexter, to the crowd in Waycross, Georgia, where he continues his recruitment for the Poor People's Campaign.

The old Cessna, with one misfiring engine, carries a nervous Doc and his excited boys all over the state as he continues to paint the picture of springtime in Washington, when an encampment of unprecedented size will awaken an indifferent nation to the plight of the poor.

When a writer wonders whether it's a good idea for Doc to be traveling in the rural South without a bodyguard, Doc waxes philosophical:

"I'd feel like a bird in a cage.... There's no way in the world you can keep somebody from killing you if they want to kill you."

Because of the malfunctioning plane, he arrives four

hours late in Augusta, where he makes his impassioned pitch for Georgians to join his grand crusade.

On a wing and a prayer, the Cessna makes it back to Atlanta. The boys are driven home to Coretta while Doc boards a late-night flight to New York so that he can arrive in time to preach a Sunday sermon in Harlem.

He's exhausted.

Aides remind him that SCLC funds are exhausted too. For all Doc's herculean efforts, recruits are not enlisting in anywhere near the number that he had hoped.

His only comfort is in sleep — and the knowledge that in a few hours he will be helping an ex-assistant and trusted friend move into a position of greater prominence. He does not envision that even this happy occasion will be marked by an ugly confrontation.

Arriving at Canaan Baptist Church, the last thing in the world Doc expects is a protest by Adam Clayton Powell, returned from Bimini and enraged at Doc and Doc's former chief of staff Wyatt Tee Walker, who this very morning is being inaugurated as pastor of the Harlem church. In a display of great loyalty, Doc has come to lend his prestige to the man with whom he shared a jail cell back in Birmingham. He sees Walker as one of his best and brightest soldiers.

Powell is incensed. He accuses Walker of luring congregants away from his own Abyssinian Baptist Church, where Walker once served as his assistant minister, before

Powell publicly fired him. In a broader attack, Powell tells the press that "the white man is finished. I don't call for violence or riots, but the day of Martin Luther King has come to an end." He insists that pacifists will never again control the black movement.

In his own press conference that day, Doc again refrains from attacking Powell. He sticks to the principles, insisting that "reasonable, meaningful non-violence" is as relevant as ever. In fact, he says, "I think it's just arrived."

The Monday meeting with SCLC staffers in Manhattan is another heartache. The same laments: the lack of money, the disagreements over the upcoming Poor People's Campaign. With all issues unresolved, Doc rushes off to a small airport where he boards a tiny one-engine for a bumpy flight to the Catskill Mountains. He's there to fulfill his promise to speak to the Sixty-Eighth Rabbinical Assembly.

"Where in America today," asks his great friend Rabbi Abraham Joshua Heschel, "do we hear a voice like the voice of the prophets of Israel? Martin Luther King is a sign that God has not forsaken the United States of America....The situation of the poor in America is our plight, our sickness. To be deaf to their cry is to condemn ourselves."

Doc uses the occasion to ask the rabbis to help him recruit volunteers for his spring crusade.

"We need bodies," he says, "to bring about the pressure to get Congress and the nation moving in the right direction."

At the evening's end, the rabbis serenade the Baptist preacher with a Hebrew version of "We Shall Overcome."

The prop plane flies him back to Manhattan, where that evening he's due for dinner at his physician Arthur Logan's home for what he hopes will be a relaxing night.

The evening is anything but relaxing. Doc engages in heavy drinking and even heavier disputations with Logan's wife, Marian, the SCLC board member vehemently opposed to his Poor People's Campaign. Her husband's attempt to change the subject falls on deaf ears. Doc can't fathom how a bright woman like Marian can't understand the urgency of his plan. Marian can't understand how a bright man like Doc can't understand its impracticality. Their argument goes on for far too long. In Marian's view, Doc is "losing hold."

*They call it stormy Monday*
*But Tuesday's just as bad*

On Tuesday, his head aching from the night before, Doc leaves the Logans' elegant East Side brownstone for a Harlem tenement, where, in a press event geared to highlight the impoverished state of urban America, he visits a welfare mother of eight, followed by a meeting with community activists, followed by an address to clergymen in Queens, followed by a speech at the Convent Avenue Baptist Church back in Harlem.

On Wednesday, he rides through the Lincoln Tunnel to New Jersey, where, in Newark, scene of last summer's calamitous riot, he meets with two dozen businessmen, asking that they back his Poor People's Campaign, before telling a rally of fourteen hundred students and teachers at the predominantly black Southside High, "Stand up with dignity and self-respect....I'm black and beautiful!"

Before leaving Newark for recruitment rallies in churches in two of the state's poorest cities—Paterson and Jersey City—Doc visits two welfare families and then pays a surprise visit to the home of LeRoi Jones (who would later change his name to Amiri Baraka), a celebrated black playwright and intellectual and an impassioned militant who has openly ridiculed Doc's pacifism. Jones is facing a weapons charge brought during last summer's Newark riots.

"Hello, LeRoi," says Doc, standing on Jones's porch. "You don't look like such a bad person. People told me you were a bad person."

The purpose of the meeting is to show Jones, one of his most vociferous critics, that Doc is willing to hear him out. Doc is also concerned that if Jones works to provoke another riot, it will impede the Poor People's Campaign.

When the press asks Jones about the meeting, his remarks are surprisingly measured. By simply listening to his adversary, Doc's loving spirit has impacted the fiery revolutionary.

"We talked about unifying the black people," Jones says with untypical humility.

Because he allows so many opponents to speak for so long, Doc is habitually late. Today is no different. After a half-dozen grueling events in New Jersey, he hurries through the Holland Tunnel and up Manhattan's West Side Highway, where, hours behind schedule, he shows up at the apartment of Harry and Julie Belafonte for a big fund-raiser party for SCLC.

In addition to supporters, there are a number of writers in attendance, including Tom Wicker and Anthony Lewis of the *New York Times*. Doc speaks eloquently about his Poor People's Campaign. But when the reporters and supporters leave, and it's just Harry, Julie, Doc, and a few of Doc's closest aides, Doc takes off his tie, kicks off his shoes, and throws back a little sherry.

His mood turns dark.

"What bothers you, Martin?" asks Harry. "What's got you in such a surly mood?"

"Newark. Beyond what an eruption in that city would mean, how it would take us off-course, I'm just so disturbed at what I'm hearing.... Frustration over the war has brought forth this idea that the solution resides in violence. What I cannot get across to these young people is that I wholly embrace everything they feel. It's just the tactics we can't agree on. I have more in common with these young people than with anybody else in the movement. I feel their rage. I feel their pain. I feel their frustration. It's the system that's the problem, and it's choking us to death!"

When Andy Young breaks in to say, "Well, I don't know, it's not the entire system. It's only part of it, and I think we can fix it," Doc loses his cool and admonishes Andy, who continues to harbor grave doubts about the Poor People's Campaign. Doc can tolerate dissent coming from those, like LeRoi Jones, who oppose him. But his patience with dissent from within his own troops is wearing thin.

"The trouble," he tells Andy, "is that we live in a failed system. Capitalism does not permit an even flow of economic resources. With this system, a small privileged few are rich beyond conscience and almost all others are doomed to be poor at some level."

Reminded that there has been success with the struggle against that system, Doc rejoins, "Yes, we've fought hard and long, and I have never doubted that we would prevail in this struggle. Already our rewards have begun to reveal themselves—desegregation, the Voting Rights Act.... But what deeply troubles me now is that for all the steps we've taken toward integration, I've come to believe that we are integrating into a burning house."

"If that's what you think, what would you have us do?" asks Harry.

His answer comes unhesitatingly:

"We...have to become firemen."


The heat is coming from Memphis.

Tomorrow—Thursday, March 28—Doc will lead the rescheduled march through the middle of Memphis.

Tonight, though, he'll catch a couple of hours of sleep before making the early morning airport run.

He'd like to take a break. He'd like to have a few days

at home, a few days away from the pressure and the press and the overstimulation of these tumultuous public demonstrations.

But there's not a chance in the world that he'll skip Memphis.

After all, he looked the strikers in the eye and gave his word.

His commitment to their cause is ironclad.

Here, at the end of another crazy, draining day of over-exertion, over-speaking, over-listening, his thoughts keep coming back to Memphis.

And here, at the break of dawn, his head throbbing, so many ideas, so many dreams, so many hopes, so many fears...

Memphis stays on his mind.

## Chapter Twenty-One

# MIDNIGHT HOUR IN MEMPHIS

The day is done.

The march is done.

Doc's world has come undone.

The moment of triumph has turned catastrophic. What should have been a peaceful march through the heart of black Memphis to the steps of city hall exploded into a full-on riot. Looters ran wild. The police moved in with Mace, nightsticks, and tear gas. A sixteen-year-old boy was shot to death by the police. Fifty other people were injured and another 120 arrested. The governor called up four thousand National Guardsmen to restore order and the mayor virtually shut down the city.

Doc has been subjected to violence during demonstrations many times before — but violence generated by angry whites. Now, for the first time, a march led by Martin

Luther King Jr. has degenerated into violence instigated by the black demonstrators themselves.

It could not have happened at a worse time.

Doc saw Memphis as the place where his leadership as a committed pacifist would be firmly restored. Memphis would show militants like LeRoi Jones how peaceful protest — in contrast to indiscriminate violence — produces remarkable results. Success in Memphis would perpetuate his Poor People's Campaign and bring in recruits by the thousands. Memphis would prove to be the glorious gateway to Washington.

Those were Doc's hopes when his plane landed an hour late and he was rushed to the Clayborn Temple African Methodist Church, where, at 11:05 a.m., six thousand citizens — the vast majority of whom were Negroes — began the march. Then, within minutes of turning onto fabled Beale Street, a group of young demonstrators, using sticks holding support-the-garbage-workers-themed signs, started smashing store windows.

As chaos broke out, Doc did not want to leave; he wanted to stay and do what he could to dissuade the rioters. But he was given no choice. Officials feared for Doc's safety and whisked him away. Unable to reach the Lorraine Motel — the police were blocking off streets in every direction — he had to be taken to the Holiday Inn Rivermont Hotel, where, some thirteen hours later, Doc is in bed, still unable to sleep, his spirit at the lowest ebb of his life.

How did it happen?

How did the hope of Memphis turn into absolute hell?

Doc has been told that the strike leadership, both among union organizers and local black preachers, was in disarray. They had not adequately prepared the marchers. They had failed to root out the militants, particularly the instigators, a group of black youth known as the Invaders.

But the cause hardly matters.

Doc is distraught. Facing defeats in his past, he has often fallen into despondency. But this time the debilitation is far deeper; the blues have rendered him inert. Fully clothed, with the covers pulled over his body, he cannot sleep yet cannot get out of bed.

Cannot imagine how his movement can possibly recover from the calamity. Cannot help but see his grand vision of a Poor People's Campaign crumbling before his very eyes. Cannot summon forth his usual reservoir of tenacity and optimism. Cannot move. Cannot be consoled.

In an attempt to reassure him that not all is lost, Doc's loyal friend Stanley Levison called him after the riot. Aware that Doc is physically and emotionally exhausted, Levison wants Doc to acknowledge that the overwhelming number of marchers remained peaceful, and that only a few had turned violent. Surely Doc can take comfort in that fact.

But comfort does not come. Levison and Abernathy and Andy Young and even Coretta cannot understand what Doc has been feeling these past weeks and months: he feels the angel of death hovering over him.

He has spoken of it time and again, but no one really wants to take his remarks about impending doom at face value. The thought is too terrible, the prospect unthinkable.

And yet the urgency that Doc has been feeling—the need to bring an army of impoverished blacks, whites, Latinos, and Native Americans to the doorstep of Congress—has been made all the more frantic by his sense of tragic fate. His insane schedule has been fueled by the certainty of his uncertain future. The Poor People's Campaign is the job and the job must get done. Now the outbreak of violence in Memphis means that the job will *not* get done. All is lost. All Doc can do is weep and pray for sleep.

The day after—Friday, March 29, 3 p.m.

Doc is still at the Holiday Inn, still struggling to maintain emotional equilibrium.

Levison calls, again trying to becalm his friend. He continues to stress all that has been accomplished and all the good that lies ahead.

His words have little effect. A political realist, Doc analyzes his situation with unsentimental clarity: yesterday's debacle will embolden the black leaders who oppose him—from Adam Clayton Powell to Stokely Carmichael to Bayard Rustin. And the whites who oppose him—from the president of the United States on down—will use this moment to attack him.

"Martin Luther King is dead," Doc tells Levison. "He's finished. His nonviolence is nothing, no one is listening to it. Let's face it, we do have a great public relations setback where my image and my leadership are concerned."

He goes on to explain that earlier in the day the Invaders—the youths who instigated the riot—turned up at his hotel.

"They came to me," says Doc. "I didn't even call for them. They came up here. They love me. They were fighting the leadership of Memphis. They were fighting Jim Lawson and the men who...would not hear them and wouldn't give them any attention....I had no knowledge of all this. I know the fellows, and they really do love me. They were too sick to see what they were doing yesterday was hurting me much more than it could hurt the local preachers. But...what do we do?"

Doc considers a fast, in the tradition of Gandhi, whose pacifist demonstrations also triggered violence. A fast would symbolize atonement.

Levison still thinks that Doc is overreacting, that he is wrong to assume the blame for a march at which 99 percent of the marchers behaved nonviolently.

It doesn't matter whether he assumes the blame or not, Doc insists, because the press will undoubtedly place the blame on him.

"Watch your newspapers," Doc tells Levison. "Watch what the *New York Times* says. It will be the most negative thing about Martin Luther King you have ever seen."

Doc is right.


The *New York Times* calls the incident "a powerful embarrassment to Dr. King" and urges him to cancel his Poor

People's Campaign: "None of the precautions he and his aides are taking to keep the capital demonstration peaceful can provide any dependable insurance against another eruption of the kind that rocked Memphis....Dr. King must by now realize that his descent on Washington is likely to prove even more counterproductive."

"King's position as leader of a nonviolent movement has been shattered," says the local Memphis paper, the *Commercial Appeal*. "He wrecked his reputation when he took off at high speed when violence occurred, instead of trying to use his persuasive prestige to stop it."

Reading such reports is infuriating, not only because of the mean-spirited animus but because of the flagrant mischaracterization of the facts.

Yet in the face of extreme adversity, Doc manages to rally.

In a press conference before leaving Memphis, he does not defend himself. Instead he takes the high road and defends SCLC. He says that contrary to published reports, "my organization had no part in planning the march. Our intelligence was totally nil."

He fights through his own sense of defeat and defiantly announces that he will soon return to the city to lead another major march—this one under the careful planning of his own people. Under no circumstances will he abandon Memphis's garbage workers. The urgency of their issues will not be ignored.

When asked whether yesterday's civil disturbance will cause him to cancel his Poor People's Campaign, he stands firm: "We are fully determined to go to Washington. We feel it is an absolute necessity."

Memphis isn't only on Doc's mind. On no fewer than three separate occasions, LBJ points to Memphis. He calls the riot a reminder that "violence and repression can only divide our people" and, borrowing a phrase from Lincoln, decries "redress by mob law." The stinging criticism of the press is one thing. But a rebuke from the president of the United States is quite another.

The blind man has hands of steel.

He requires all the strength at his command to undo the dense knots in Doc's aching back and neck. The masseur at Atlanta's downtown YMCA has worked on Doc many times before, but he has never felt anything like the muscular tightness that he must manipulate today.

Just off the plane from Memphis, Doc is on the rubdown table. He prizes the skill of the sightless man to attack his tension. The fact that the massage therapist works in complete silence is an extra bonus. Aimless chatter is the last thing in the world that Doc wants to hear.

Doc wants to lose consciousness of all thought and analysis; wants to cease reviewing the past week and the past month and the past year; wants to stop anticipating what will happen today and tomorrow and the day after tomorrow; wants to stop pursuing and planning and putting on a brave face before those who doubt him or those who would destroy him; wants to stop fearing the destruction of his grand vision; wants to stop fearing his own death; wants to stop the endless rotation of complex ideas and ugly images that have been haunting him night and day; wants to find relief in this mindless act of lying supine on a massage table and allowing the relief that comes when muscles are untangled and thoughts disappear.

An avalanche of thoughts returns the next day—Saturday, March 30—at an SCLC emergency meeting at Ebenezer. The emergency, of course, is Memphis.

In the wake of the riot, Doc's hope is that his closest colleagues will support his commitment to redouble his efforts to back the strikers. He needs SCLC to reaffirm his mission.

It doesn't happen. Instead he faces more biting criticism and bickering dissent.

Why did Doc agree to participate in the march without being certain that the Memphis leaders had the militants under control?

And why in the world does he want to go back?

Forget Memphis. Memphis was a bust. Memphis continues to be not only a distraction but a draining misadventure. It's time to move on from Memphis.

Doc will not move on. He argues that the principles—and pragmatism—of pacifism must be reestablished. "Memphis is the Washington campaign in miniature," he claims. Memphis must be made right so supporters can see the positive prospects of occupying the capital.

But SCLC insiders do more than attack Doc's association with Memphis; they attack the efficacy of his Poor People's Campaign, period.

Andy Young states unequivocally that if the campaign does take place, it must be delayed for at least a year.

Stanley Levison rejects Doc's argument that the campaign will be analogous to the bonus marchers of the Great Depression. Like other King advisers, he doubts the campaign's political wisdom.

James Bevel is vehemently against the entire operation. "We don't need to be hanging around Washington," he insists. "We need to stop this war."

Jesse Jackson thinks that the Memphis situation is too small to merit Doc's attention and the Poor People's Campaign too unorganized. Jackson wants attention focused on his Operation Breadbasket.

Doc snaps. He's heard enough.

He accuses Young of capitulating to his doubts.

He accuses Bevel of capitulating to the paralysis of analysis.

He accuses Jackson of capitulating to his own ambition.

He storms out of the meeting.

His aides run after him.

"Doc, Doc, don't worry! Everything's going to be all right," Jackson shouts.

"Jesse," Doc answers, "everything's *not* going to be all right! If things keep going the way they're going now, it's not SCLC but the whole country that's in trouble.... If you're so interested in doing your own thing that you can't do what this organization's structured to do, if you want to carve out your own niche in society, go ahead. But for God's sake, don't bother me!"

Ralph Abernathy has never seen Doc this agitated. Walking him to his car, Abernathy expresses his deep concern for his friend's well-being.

"I'll snap out of it," Doc mutters. "I'll pull through it."

Doc gets in the car and, rejecting all company — even the companionship of his friend Ralph — he does something he rarely does, especially in light of an ever-increasing number of threats to his life.

He drives off into the night.

Alone.

With no word about where he is going.

## Chapter Twenty-Two

# FREEDOM EXPLOSION

The next day, the preacher can be found back in the pulpit.

It is the last Sunday in March, and Doc is using his sermon at Washington National Cathedral to lift his own spirits.

Determined to fight the despondency dragging him down, he looks to one of the brightest passages in the Book of Revelation: "Behold, I make all things new; former things are passed away."

He points out how, just as Rip van Winkle slept through the American Revolution, there are those among the parishioners sleeping through the day's revolution. There are those among them missing all that is new. The new and most compelling revolution is the one for human rights, "the freedom explosion that is taking place all over the world."

That revolution will not wait. It will not slow down for

those who claim that progressives like Doc are moving too quickly. It will not be quieted by those who claim that "the Negro must lift himself by his own bootstraps."

These antirevolutionaries "never stop to realize that no other ethnic group has been a slave on American soil.... It's all right to tell a man to lift himself by his own bootstraps, but it is a cruel jest to say to a bootless man that he ought to lift himself by his own bootstraps."

Doc links racism to the issue that allows him no peace: poverty.

"Like a monstrous octopus, poverty spreads its nagging, prehensile tentacles into hamlets and villages all over our world. Two-thirds of the people of the world go to bed hungry tonight. They are ill-housed; they are ill-nourished; they are shabbily clad. I've seen it in Latin America; I've seen it in Africa; I've seen this poverty in Asia."

Doc brings the message home to America, speaking about his trip to Marks, Mississippi. "I saw hundreds of little black boys and black girls walking the streets with no shoes to wear. I saw their mothers and fathers trying to carry on a little Head Start program, but they had no money."

He speaks of his recent visits to the tenements of Newark and Harlem and the frustrations that he faces as a man determined to force the country he loves to heed the cries of the dispossessed.

And, of course, he speaks of his Poor People's Campaign.

"In a few weeks some of us are coming to Washington

to see if the will is still alive...in this nation....Yes, we are going to bring the tired, the poor, the huddled masses.... We are going to bring those who have come to feel that life is a long and desolate corridor with no exit signs. We are going to bring children and adults and old people, people who have never seen a doctor or a dentist....

"We are not coming to engage in any histrionic gesture. We are not coming to tear up Washington....We are coming to ask America to be true to the huge promissory note that it signed years ago," he urges, repeating the admonition that he first articulated during his "I Have a Dream" speech five years earlier.

"We are coming," he continues, "to engage in dramatic nonviolent action, to call attention to the gulf between the promise and fulfillment; to make the invisible visible."

Doc makes visible his most vehement critics by telling the story of a newsman who confronted him:

"Dr. King," he asked, "don't you think you're going to have to stop, now, opposing the war and move more in line with the administration's policy?...It has hurt the budget of your organization, and people who once respected you have lost respect for you."

"I'm not a consensus leader," Doc replied. "I do not determine what is right and wrong by looking at the budget of the Southern Christian Leadership Conference."

"Ultimately," Doc tells his congregants, "a genuine leader is not a searcher for consensus, but a molder of consensus.

"Cowardice asks the question — *is it safe?* Expedience

asks the question — *is it politic?* Vanity asks the question — *is it popular?* Conscience asks the question — *is it right?*"

Doc closes by declaring that he will not "yield to a politic of despair. I'm going to maintain hope as we come to Washington in this campaign. The cards are stacked against us. This time we will really confront a Goliath. God grant that we will be that David of truth set out against the Goliath of injustice, the Goliath of neglect....

"Our goal is freedom, and I believe we are going to get there because however much she strays away from it, the goal of America is freedom. Abused and scorned though we may be as a people, our destiny is tied up in the destiny of America."

But what of Doc's destiny?

Even before the Memphis riot, the FBI has been working overtime to undermine him. On one front, it issued fraudulent news leaks in the North about how SCLC, flush with cash, was not in need of funds. Meanwhile, FBI agents wrote letters to supporters in the South saying that there was "no provision to house or feed marchers" in the upcoming Washington campaign, whose purpose was only "King's personal aggrandizement."

"Prepare the letters on commercially purchased stationery," J. Edgar Hoover instructed his underlings, "and take all necessary precautions to insure they cannot be traced back to the Bureau."

After Memphis, the bureau's anti-King campaign grew even nastier. A memo was sent to the media claiming that "the result of King's famous espousal of nonviolence was vandalism, looting, and riot." Doc was seen as "like Judas leading lambs to slaughter." Hoover told his friends in the press that "King led the marchers to violence, and when the violence broke out, King disappeared." Rather than go to the Lorraine, "owned and patronized exclusively by Negroes," Doc preferred "the plush Holiday Inn Motel, white owned, operated, and almost exclusively white patronized."

Doc knows nothing about these assaults on his character and campaign. He does know, however, that the upcoming presidential elections will have an enormous impact on the poor.

With that in mind, on the Sunday afternoon following his Washington National Cathedral sermon, Doc and Andy Young meet with Michigan congressman John Conyers and Gary, Indiana, mayor Richard Hatcher to discuss which of the candidates—Eugene McCarthy or Bobby Kennedy— might better serve the needs of the underprivileged. Either way, Doc is vehemently opposed to the renomination of President Johnson.

Even in the midst of the political discussion, though, Doc is still clearly caught up in a state of dejection.

"I don't know when I have ever seen him as discouraged and depressed," Young will later say.

Sunday evening Doc watches the president address the nation. The shock of Johnson's announcement changes Doc's dark mood, if only for the moment:

"I shall not seek and I will not accept the nomination of my party as your President."

The statement is startling. No one expected Johnson to leave the race. It is, in some respects, a victory for those who, like Doc, have tirelessly opposed his war policy. It is recognition of the reality that such a policy has rendered LBJ politically impotent.

Doc is gratified that, adhering to the hawks, Johnson cannot sustain his presidency. At the same time, Doc's heart cannot help but feel for a man who courageously supported the cause of racial equality.

In 1963, shortly after the assassination of John Kennedy, it was Johnson who turned to Doc to offer support for his cause.

In 1965, after the riots broke out in Watts, it was Johnson who called Doc to gain a deeper understanding of the disturbance.

And, of course, it was Johnson who invited Doc to the White House on many occasions, not only to personally confer with the president but to witness the signing of the historic legislation that the two allies—the shrewd politician from Texas and the Baptist preacher from Georgia—labored long and hard to bring to life: the Civil Rights Act of 1964 and the Voting Rights Act of 1965.

Doc remembers that it was Johnson who, addressing the cause of black Americans, said, "Let us close the springs of racial poison. Let us pray for wise and understanding hearts. Let us lay aside irrelevant differences."

And yet other essential and earth-shattering differences cannot be set aside:

Johnson pursues a war that Doc considers one of the great disasters of American history. Through his FBI director, Johnson is aggressively working to decimate Doc's effort to activate his Poor People's Campaign. Even as Johnson's political currency is on the verge of bankruptcy, the president's minions are manipulating the media to demonize Doc and destroy his plans.

On this last day of March, the day of Lyndon Johnson's surprise statement about his political future, Doc has no choice but to focus on the future of his own political plans.

The future is obviously not about LBJ.

Nor is the future about a futile attempt to win an unwinnable war.

In Doc's mind, the future continues to be about one place, and one place only.

Memphis.

*Chapter Twenty-Three*

# THE MOUNTAINTOP IN MEMPHIS

Fate is a mysterious thing.

On the morning of Wednesday, April 3, Mable John, a soul singer who lives in Chicago, makes a fateful decision to give up her room at the Lorraine Motel—number 306—to Dr. Martin Luther King Jr.

A recording star for Memphis's Stax Records, Mable has been in the studio cutting a new album, even as her current single—"Able Mable"—is being played on WDIA. The sessions have been extended a few days longer than anticipated, thus delaying her departure.

Walter Bailey, the Lorraine's owner, tells Mable that Dr. King is coming to town to lead another march next Monday on behalf of the striking garbage workers. Would she mind vacating her room—Doc's favorite—and moving to another?

Mable doesn't mind at all. She's known and admired

Doc for many years. When she sees him checking in shortly after 11 a.m., they exchange warm greetings.

"Will you be preaching while you're here, Dr. King?" she asks.

"More marching than preaching, Mable," he says. "Caught something of a sore throat."

Mable hears that his voice is scratchy and sees that his eyes are filled with fatigue.

"The flight coming in was a little rough," he says.

"Stormy weather all around."

"That, and a bomb scare back in Atlanta. Delayed the flight nearly two hours."

"Mercy!" exclaims Mable.

"I was just grateful that they found out about the threat *before* we took off."

"You need to be careful, Dr. King. You need to take good care."

"I'm in the best care, Mable," he says. "I'm in God's care."

"I just pray to God to keep you safe."

"He always has, and He always will," says Doc. "His love is the only safety we need."

"I know that's right."

"Be sure and send me your new record," he says.

"I sure will. I'll be honored for you to hear it."

As Mable leaves for the recording studio, Doc and his entourage — Ralph Abernathy, Andy Young, Jesse Jackson, Dorothy Cotton, James Bevel, Bernard Lee — go to their rooms to unpack. Doc and Abernathy share room 306.

Outside, a detail of police cruisers, sent by the city to protect the preacher, encircle the Lorraine.

An hour later, Doc and company drive to James Lawson's church and meet with a group of black ministers to discuss Monday's march. Doc is more interested, however, in meeting with the Invaders, the militants with whom he established rapport last week.

Back at the Lorraine, the Invaders come to Doc's room, where the discussion is long and fruitful. The young men are moved not only by the minister's concern for their grievances but by the sincerity of his interest in their history. This time they vow to commit to a peaceful march and assure Doc that they will monitor the demonstrators, making sure that all agitators—especially the ones engaged by hostile forces like the FBI to wreak havoc—are subdued. Doc is deeply gratified to accept their pledge of solidarity.

He feels Memphis turning his way. Only here in Memphis has he finally been able to build a bridge to the militants, a longtime dream come true.

In the middle of the meeting, though, the dream is disturbed by a loud knock on the door. Doc is served notice that the city has banned any march pending approval by a U.S. district court judge. Unless the judge lifts the ban, Monday's demonstration will be deemed illegal.

Doc's response is quick:

"We are not going to be stopped by Mace or injunctions."

In short order, members of his staff, along with ACLU

lawyers, put together a legal response, setting up a hearing for the following day.

The fact that the power structure has thrown a roadblock in his path does not discourage Doc. Opposition from outside forces is something that he has long learned to navigate. Far more painful has been opposition from his own people, especially the youth. Thus the rapprochement with the Invaders is especially heartening.

The weather is not heartening. The pathetic fallacy is back in play. The early evening sky is an ominous mix of darkness and light. Tornadoes have touched down in neighboring counties. A storm warning is in effect. Walking out of his second-story room onto the balcony, Doc looks out into the distance. He sees jagged bolts of lightning. He hears the crack and rumble of rolling thunder.

The bomb scare, the flight from Atlanta, the meeting with the Invaders, the court injunction—the day's events have worn him out. He thinks of the rally that has been set up tonight for the strikers at Mason Temple and decides not to go. Even if it isn't postponed due to tornado warnings, few people will brave going out on a night such as this.

Back in his room, he calls Coretta in Atlanta. In spite of everything, he characterizes the day as "good." He tells her that he loves her. He asks that she kiss the kids for him.

He tells Abernathy that if, in fact, the rally takes place, he, Ralph, should speak for him.

Ralph, in turn, suggests that Jesse Jackson address the strikers.

Doc agrees that Jackson can come along but insists that Ralph do the speaking.

Despite the weather, the rally does go on. While Doc rests in his room, Abernathy makes his way to the great hall, where he is surprised to see that, in spite of the stormy night, there is a decent crowd. Everyone is saying the same thing:

*Where is Dr. King?*

*When will Dr. King be here?*

*We have to hear from Dr. King.*

Abernathy hurries into the hallway, where he picks up a pay phone and calls the Lorraine.

"Room 306," he tells the desk clerk.

The phone keeps ringing. Abernathy fears that Doc has already fallen asleep and won't respond. He lets the phone keep ringing. Finally, his weary friend lifts the receiver.

Wasting no time, Abernathy lets Doc know that there is no way that this assembly will be satisfied until Martin Luther King Jr. stands before them and says a few words. On one of the nastiest nights of the year, this crowd has braved the storm. People are here because they need inspiration. Along with their wives, girlfriends, sisters, brothers, mothers, and fathers, the garbage workers have come en masse. They're not leaving until Doc shows up and lets them know that we shall overcome.

Doc is moved. He shakes the sleepiness from his eyes, puts on his customary coat and tie, and is driven through the rain to Mason Temple, where he is greeted with a tumultuous ovation.

As a torrential thunderstorm cracks open and pelts the hall with a pounding rain, Abernathy gives a laudatory introduction, setting up the expectation that Doc has come tonight to do more than merely say a few words. He has come to preach.

"His daddy is a preacher," says Abernathy. "His granddaddy was a preacher. His uncle was a preacher. His brother is a preacher, and of course his dearest friend and other brother" — a self-reference — "is one of the world's greatest preachers!"

Doc is indeed ready to preach, ready to purge himself of whatever doubts and fears, whatever despondency and darkness, have threatened him in these past days, weeks, and months.

Like the blues player embracing his guitar or the jazz musician taking up his horn, Doc comes to the pulpit to sing himself out of sadness; he comes to the pulpit to testify to the truth of his conviction; he comes to raise his own wounded spirits even as he raises the spirits of those fighting for their livelihood.

He comes to say that were he standing at the beginning of time and God Almighty asked him which epoch he'd like to live in, he'd tell the Lord, Let me live in ancient Egypt and ancient Rome; let me live in the ages of the Renaissance and the Reformation; let me live through the American Civil War and World War II. But most pointedly, he'd say to the Lord, "If you allow me to live just a few years in the second half of the twentieth century, I will be happy."

Even though today "the world is all messed up. The nation is sick. Trouble is in the land, confusion all around," he is grateful to be right where he is.

In this very moment.

In Memphis.

He preaches, "I'm just happy that God has allowed me to live in this period, to see what is unfolding. And I'm happy that He's allowed me to be in Memphis."

Happy to be alive.

He thinks back to recent times, when "Negroes were just going around...scratching where they didn't itch, and laughing when they were not tickled. But that day is all over. We mean business now, and we are determined to gain our rightful place in God's world....

"The issue is injustice. The issue is the refusal of Memphis to be fair and honest in its dealings with its public servants, who happen to be sanitation workers....

"Now we're going to march again, and we've got to march again, in order to...force everybody to see that there are thirteen hundred of God's children here suffering, sometimes going hungry, going through dark and dreary nights wondering how this thing is going to come out.... For when people get caught up with that which is right and they are willing to sacrifice for it, there is no stopping point short of victory."

Doc goes on to list the victories in Birmingham, where the fire hoses and the dogs couldn't stop them; where right defeated might; where the words they sang—"Over my head, I see freedom in the air"—sustained the spirit of hope and love, disarming those wielding deadly weapons.

Doc preaches that nonviolence remains the most potent weapon.

"We don't have to argue with anybody," he says. "We don't have to curse and go around acting bad with our words. We don't need any bricks and bottles. We don't need any Molotov cocktails. We just need to go around to these... massive industries in our country and say, 'God sent us by here to say to you that you're not treating His children right. And we've come by here to ask you to make the first item on your agenda fair treatment.... Now, if you are not prepared to do that, we do have an agenda that we must follow. And our agenda calls for withdrawing economic support from you.'"

But tonight, Doc's agenda transcends economic analysis. Tonight mortality is on his mind. His own.

He tells the story of how, in 1958, a "demented woman" stabbed him in Harlem during a book signing.

"The tip of the blade was on the edge of my aorta, the main artery," he says. "If I had merely sneezed, I would have died....

"I want to say tonight that I...am happy that I didn't sneeze. Because if I had sneezed, I wouldn't have been around here in 1960, when students all over the South started sitting in at lunch counters....

"If I had sneezed, I wouldn't have been around here in

1962, when Negroes in Albany, Georgia, decided to straighten their backs up. And whenever men and women straighten their backs up, they are going somewhere, because a man can't ride your back unless it is bent....

"If I had sneezed, I wouldn't have been here in 1963, when the black people of Birmingham, Alabama, aroused the conscience of this nation and brought into being the civil rights bill.

"If I had sneezed, I wouldn't have had a chance later that year, in August, to try to tell America about a dream that I had had.

"If I had sneezed, I wouldn't have been down in Selma, Alabama, to see the great movement there.

"If I had sneezed, I wouldn't have been in Memphis to see a community rally around those brothers and sisters who are suffering.

"I'm so happy that I didn't sneeze."

He goes deeper into the notion of his near death. He speaks of the bomb scare in Atlanta that very morning. He speaks of the threats to his life right there in Memphis, about "what would happen to me from some of our sick white brothers," and then about strength.

"Just as I say, we aren't going to let dogs or water hoses turn us around. We aren't going to let any injunction turn us around....

"Well, I don't know what will happen now. We've got some difficult days ahead. But it really doesn't matter with me now, because I've been to the mountaintop. And I don't mind. Like anybody, I would like to live a long life. Longevity has its place. But I'm not concerned about that now. I just want to do God's will.

"And He's allowed me to go up to the mountain.

"And I've looked over.

"And I've seen the promised land.

"I may not get there with you. But I want you to know tonight that we, as a people, will get to the promised land!

"And so I'm happy tonight.

"I'm not worried about anything.

"I'm not fearing any man!

"Mine eyes have seen the glory of the coming of the Lord!"

## Chapter Twenty-Four

# APRIL 4, 1968

Exactly one year ago today, Doc stood in the pulpit of the Riverside Church and denounced President Johnson's escalating war in Vietnam.

Since then, a national poll indicates that nearly three-quarters of the American people have turned against Doc, and 57 percent of his own people consider him irrelevant.

Today, a Thursday, Doc is at the Lorraine in Memphis, getting a late start. Last night's rally did him a world of good. After collapsing in a chair on stage, he managed to attend a small post-rally get-together at the hotel. He was elated to see that his brother, A. D., had driven to the city with two women, one of whom was Georgia Davis, the state senator from Kentucky.

There was talk about the legal maneuvers to stop next week's demonstration. The women wanted to know whether Doc was considering canceling.

"The decision has been made to march," he said. "Regardless of the outcome of today's hearing, we will march on Monday. We cannot give in now."

When asked whether he was afraid for his life, his answer was chilling: "I'd rather be dead than afraid."

The talk turned to Davis's first term as a senator. Doc was keen to learn of her accomplishments. She, in turn, wanted to hear details of his recent rallies, especially the one at Mason Temple that, due to her late arrival, she had missed. It was evident that Doc and Davis had missed each other's company, and after a while, they excused themselves from the party to spend time alone.

Now it is early afternoon and Doc is feeling refreshed. While his aides are in court arguing for the legalization of Monday's march, he calls Dora McDonald, his secretary in Atlanta, to share his sermon topic for next Sunday's service at Ebenezer so that she can get it into the church bulletin. His theme is one that has been resonating in his head and heart for the past twelve months:

*Why America may go to hell.*

The topic is somber, but today Doc is not. Today he's joyful.

Today he's taking it easy.

Enjoying a catfish lunch with Ralph Abernathy.

Hanging out in A. D.'s room.

Calling home.

Chatting with Mom and Dad.

Feeling the happiness that his parents experience when they know their sons are together.

Telling his folks that he loves them.

Assuring Mama King and Daddy King that all's well in Memphis.

Claiming that victory is at hand.

Kidding around with Andy Young when he walks through the door.

"Li'l nigger," says Doc lovingly, "where you been?"

Doc knows that Andy's been to court to testify about the peaceful preparations for Monday's March, but Doc wants to forget politics—at least for now. Doc wants to play. He and Ralph grab pillows and start going after Andy. Grown men acting like little boys. The pillow fight has everyone laughing.

Everyone is looking forward to tonight's early dinner at the home of Reverend Billy Kyles.

Looking forward to a soul food feast.

Learning from Billy's wife, Gwen, all the items on the menu: everything from chitterlings to neck bones to turnip greens to cornbread.

Doc's hungry.

Doc's happy.

Doc's hearing music coming from downstairs, where Jesse Jackson is rehearsing an ensemble of Operation Breadbasket singing hymns like "I'm So Glad (Trouble Don't Last Always)."

Doc greets Billy Kyles, who has arrived at his room intending to drive him over to his home. It's nearly 6 p.m.

Doc's still in jokester mode.

"Now Billy," he says, "if you've bought this big new

house and can't afford to feed us, I'm gonna tell everybody in the country."

Kyles assures him that there will be more than enough good food to go around.

Doc keeps joking: "Your wife can't cook, anyway. She's too good-looking."

The two men step outside, on the balcony. In the wake of yesterday's storm, the air is clean and fresh.

Kyles heads down to the car.

Doc leans over the rail. Takes a deep breath. Spots Jesse Jackson in the courtyard.

"Jesse," Doc yells down, "I want you to come to dinner with me."

Jesse introduces Doc to the man standing next to him.

"Doc, you remember Ben Branch? He's our saxophonist. Memphis musician."

"Oh, yes," Doc calls down, "he's my man. How are you, Ben?...Make sure you play 'Precious Lord, Take My Hand' in the meeting tonight. Play it real pretty."

Then a shot rings out.

The bullet finds its mark.

Doc falls.


At age thirty-nine, his life on earth ends.

# EPILOGUE

Three years earlier, in March 1965, Doc told the White House that, no, he could not accept an invitation to a joint session of Congress where the president was introducing the Voting Rights Act. Doc had worked tirelessly for the legislation, but his heart led him to Brown Chapel in Selma, Alabama. There he delivered a eulogy for Reverend James Joseph Reeb, a white man who had become a Quaker social worker in the Boston tenements before joining SCLC's campaign. While marching for civil rights, Reeb was attacked and murdered on the streets of Selma.

Doc began the eulogy with lines from Shakespeare's *Romeo and Juliet*.

*And if he should die,*
*Take his body, and cut it into little stars.*
*He will make the face of heaven so fine*
*That all the world will be in love with night.*

"These beautiful words... so eloquently describe the radiant life of James Reeb. He entered the stage of history just thirty-eight years ago, and in the brief years that he was privileged to act on this mortal stage, he played his part exceedingly well. James Reeb was martyred in the Judeo-Christian faith that all men are brothers. His death was a result of a sensitive religious spirit. His crime was that he dared to live his faith; he placed himself alongside the disinherited black brethren of this community....

"Naturally, we are compelled to ask the question, *Who* killed James Reeb? The answer is simple and rather limited, when we think of the *who*. He was murdered by a few, sick, demented, and misguided men who have the strange notion that you express dissent through murder. There is another haunting, poignant, desperate question we are forced to ask this afternoon.... It is the question, *What* killed James Reeb? When we move from the who to the what, the blame is wide and the responsibility grows.

"James Reeb was murdered by the indifference of every minister of the gospel who has remained silent behind the safe security of stained glass windows....

"He was murdered by the irresponsibility of every politician who has moved down the path of demagoguery, who has fed his constituents the stale bread of hatred and the spoiled meat of racism. He was murdered by the brutality of every sheriff and law enforcement agent who practices lawlessness in the name of law. He was murdered by the timidity of a federal government that can spend millions of dollars... in South Vietnam, yet cannot protect the lives of its own citizens seeking constitutional rights. Yes, he was even murdered by the cowardice of every Negro who tacitly accepts the evil system of segregation, who stands on the sidelines in the midst of a mighty struggle for justice.

"So in his death, James Reeb says something to each of us, black and white alike — says that we must substitute courage for caution, says to us that we must be concerned not merely about who murdered him, but about the system, the way of life, the philosophy which produced the murder. His death says to us that we must work passionately, unrelentingly, to make the American dream a reality, so he did not die in vain. . . .

"So in spite of the darkness of this hour, we must not despair. . . . We must not become bitter nor must we harbor the desire to retaliate with violence; we must not lose faith in our white brothers who happen to be misguided. Somehow we must still believe that the most misguided among them will learn to respect the dignity and worth of all human personalities. . . .

"So we thank God for the life of James Reeb. We thank God for his goodness. We thank God that he was willing to lay down his life in order to redeem the soul of our nation. So I say — so Horatio said as he stood over the dead body of Hamlet — 'Good night sweet prince: may the flight of angels take thee to thy eternal rest.'"

# ACKNOWLEDGMENTS

What a blessing to have David Ritz as a collaborator on this particular book project, which has meant more to me than any I have ever done, given my deep and abiding love for Martin Luther King Jr.

I was also blessed to have a wonderful researcher for this text, Jared Hernandez, who had boundless energy and great ideas. Without David and Jared, this text simply would not exist.

Thanks to Dr. Cornel West for the countless conversations over many years about how to make to the world safe for the legacy of Dr. King.

Deep gratitude to our leader, Michael Pietsch; my publisher, Reagan Arthur; my brilliant editor, John Parsley; the delightful Malin von Euler-Hogan; my able executive assistant, Kimberly McFarland; the indefatigable agents David Vigliano and Ken Browning; and all my friends (too numerous to count) who reviewed various parts of this manuscript in process.

Finally, to the King family I've had the pleasure of knowing, loving, and serving: Coretta Scott King, Yolanda Denise King, Martin L. King III, Dexter Scott King, and Bernice A. King. Thank you for sharing; thank you for your sacrifice.

*—Tavis Smiley*

My thanks to Tavis Smiley, whose rich mind, boundless enthusiasm, and loving dedication to this work have inspired and blessed me mightily.

Jared Hernandez, a fabulous researcher.

Roberta Ritz, whose editorial acumen is always invaluable.

David Vigliano, whose creative mind initiated this project.

John Parsley, for superb editing and total support.

Kimberly McFarland and Malin von Euler-Hogan, for ongoing encouragement.

My family: Roberta, Alison, Jessica, Jim, Henry, Charlotte, Nino, James, Isaac, sisters Elizabeth and Esther.

My friends: Harry Weinger, Alan Eisenstock, Herb Powell, John Tayloe, and all the Tuesday gang of poets and prophets.

*—David Ritz*

# SOURCES AND BIBLIOGRAPHIES

*Interviews conducted for this book:*

Belafonte, Harry

Branch, Taylor

Carson, Clayborne

Cotton, Dorothy

Garrow, David

Ghaemi, Nassir

Gregory, Dick

Harding, Vincent

Jackson, Jesse

John, Mable

Jones, Clarence

King, Coretta Scott

Kyles, Billy

Moore, Sam

Nash, Diane

Newcombe, Don

Taylor, Gardner C.

Walker, Wyatt Tee

Young, Andrew

## Texts:

Ali, Muhammad, with Richard Durham. *The Greatest: My Own Story.* New York: Random House, 1975.

Baez, Joan. *And a Voice to Sing With: A Memoir.* New York: Simon & Schuster, 1987.

Bagley, Edythe Scott. *Desert Rose: The Life and Legacy of Coretta Scott King.* Tuscaloosa: The University of Alabama Press, 2012.

Baldwin, Lewis V. *To Make the Wounded Whole: The Cultural Legacy of Martin Luther King, Jr.* Minneapolis: Augsburg Fortress, 1992.

Belafonte, Harry, with Michael Shnayerson. *My Song: A Memoir.* New York: Knopf, 2011.

Branch, Taylor. *At Canaan's Edge: America in the King Years, 1965– 68.* New York: Simon & Schuster, 2006.

———. *Parting the Waters: America in the King Years, 1954–63.* New York: Simon & Schuster, 1988.

Carson, Clayborne, ed. *The Autobiography of Martin Luther King, Jr.* New York: Warner Books, 1998.

Carmichael, Stokely. "Let Another World Be Born: Text of Speech at the Spring Mobilization to End the War in Vietnam Outside the United Nations." New York City, April 15, 1967.

Churchill, Ward, and Jim Vander Wall. *Agents of Repression: The FBI's Secret Wars Against the Black Panther Party and the American Indian Movement.* Cambridge: South End Press, 2002.

D'Emilio, John. *Lost Prophet: The Life and Times of Bayard Rustin.* New York: Free Press, 2003.

Dyson, Michael Eric. *I May Not Get There with You: The True Martin Luther King, Jr.* New York: Simon & Schuster, 2000.

Fairclough, Adam. *To Redeem the Soul of America: The Southern Christian Leadership Conference and Martin Luther King, Jr.* Athens: University of Georgia Press, 2001.

Frady, Marshall. *Martin Luther King, Jr.: A Life.* New York: Penguin Group, 2002.

Garrow, David J. *Bearing the Cross: Martin Luther King, Jr., and the Southern Christian Leadership Conference.* New York: HarperCollins, 1986.

————. *The FBI and Martin Luther King, Jr.: From "Solo" to Memphis.* New York: W. W. Norton & Company, 1981.

Ghaemi, Nassir. *A First-Rate Madness: Uncovering the Links Between Leadership and Mental Illness.* New York: Penguin Group, 2011.

Hamilton, Charles V. *Adam Clayton Powell, Jr.: The Political Biography of an American Dilemma.* New York: Cooper Square Press, 1991.

Honey, Michael K. *Going Down Jericho Road: The Memphis Strike, Martin Luther King's Last Campaign.* New York: W. W. Norton & Company, 2011.

Johnson, Lyndon B. "Address After Ordering Federal Troops to Detroit, Michigan." July 24, 1967. MillerCenter.org.

————. "Speech to the Nation on Civil Disorders." July 27, 1967. MillerCenter.org.

King, Jr., Dr. Martin Luther. "A Proper Sense of Priorities." Speech to CALCAV'S Final Plenary, New York Avenue Presbyterian, Washington, DC, February 6, 1968.

————. "Address at a Mass Meeting." Maggie Street Baptist Church, Montgomery, AL, February 16, 1968.

————. "Address to the National Association of Radio Announcers." Atlanta, GA, August 11, 1967. Transcribed from YouTube. com.

————. "The Drum Major Instinct." Sermon at Ebenezer Baptist Church, Atlanta, GA, February 4, 1968.

————. "Honoring Dr. Du Bois." Speech at Carnegie Hall, New York, NY, February 23, 1968.

————. "I Have a Dream." Speech delivered from the Lincoln Memorial in Washington, DC, August 28, 1963.

————. "The Other America." Speech at Grosse Pointe High School, Grosse Pointe, MI, March 14, 1968.

————. "Pre-Washington Campaign." Sermon at Tabernacle Baptist Church, Selma, AL, February 16, 1968.

————. "Remaining Awake Through a Great Revolution." Sermon at National Cathedral, Washington, DC, March 31, 1968.

————. "The Role of the Behavioral Scientist in the Civil Rights Movement." Address to American Psychological Association, Hilton Hotel, Washington, DC, September 1, 1967.

————. Speech at Disneyland Hotel, Anaheim, CA, March 16, 1968.

————. Speech at Mason Temple, Memphis, TN, March 18, 1968.

————. "The State of the Movement," also referred to as "A New Sense of Direction." Speech at SCLC Retreat in Frogmore, SC, November 28, 1967.

———. "Unfulfilled Dreams." Sermon at Ebenezer Baptist Church, Atlanta, GA, March 3, 1968.

———. *Where Do We Go from Here: Chaos or Community?* New York: Harper & Row, 1967.

———. "Who Is My Neighbor?" Sermon at Ebenezer Baptist Church, Atlanta, GA, February 18, 1968.

———. "Why Jesus Called a Man a Fool." Sermon at Mount Pisgah Missionary Baptist Church, Chicago, IL, August 27, 1967.

Kotz, Nick. *A Passion for Equality: George A. Wiley and the Movement.* New York: W. W. Norton, 1979.

Lefever, Harry G. *Undaunted by the Fight: Spelman College and the Civil Rights Movement, 1957–1967.* Macon: Mercer University Press, 2005.

Lincoln, C. Eric, ed. *Martin Luther King, Jr.: A Profile.* New York: Macmillan, 1984.

Longfellow, Henry Wadsworth. "Snow-flakes," in *Poems and Other Writings.* New York: Library of America, 2000.

Paris, Peter, et al. *The History of the Riverside Church in the City of New York.* New York and London: New York University Press, 2004.

Posner, Gerald. *Killing the Dream: James Earl Ray and the Assassination of Martin Luther King, Jr.* New York: Mariner Books, 1999.

Powell, Jr., Adam Clayton. *Adam by Adam: The Autobiography of Adam Clayton Powell, Jr.* New York: Kensington Publishing Group, 1971.

Powers, Georgia Davis. *I Shared the Dream: The Pride, Passion and Politics of the First Black Woman Senator from Kentucky.* Far Hills, NJ: New Horizon Press, 1995.

"Re: Martin Luther King, Jr." United States Department of Justice, Federal Bureau of Investigation, Detroit, Michigan, March 15, 1968.

Rieder, Jonathan. *The Word of the Lord Is upon Me: The Righteous Performance of Martin Luther King, Jr.* Cambridge: Harvard University Press, 2008.

Savage, Sean J. *JFK, LBJ, and the Democratic Party.* Albany: SUNY Press, 2012.

Sides, Hampton. *Hellhound on His Trail: The Electrifying Account of the Largest Manhunt in American History.* New York: Doubleday, 2010.

"Summary of March Twenty-Eight Activities: Sanitation Workers Strike, Memphis, Tennessee." Federal Bureau of Investigation, Memphis, April 12, 1968.

Theoharis, Jeanne. *The Rebellious Life of Mrs. Rosa Parks.* Boston: Beacon Press, 2013.

Wagner, Heather Lehr. *Aretha Franklin: Singer.* New York: Chelsea House, 2010.

Washington, James M., ed. *A Testament of Hope: The Essential Writings and Speeches of Martin Luther King, Jr.* New York: Harper One, 1986.

Williams, Juan. *My Soul Looks Back in Wonder: Voices of the Civil Rights Experience.* New York: Sterling Publishing Co., 2005.

———. *Thurgood Marshall: American Revolutionary.* New York: Random House: 1998.

Winkler, Adam. *Gunfight: The Battle Over the Right to Bear Arms in America.* New York: W. W. Norton & Company, 2011.

Woodard, Komozi. *A Nation Within a Nation: Amiri Baraka (LeRoi Jones) and Black Power Politics.* Chapel Hill: University of North Carolina Press, 1999.

Young, Andrew. *An Easy Burden: The Civil Rights Movement and the Transformation of America.* Waco: Baylor University Press: 2008.

## *Newspaper & Magazine Articles:*

"A Tragedy." *Washington Post,* April 6, 1967: 20.

Adler, Renata. "Letter from the Palmer House." *The New Yorker,* September 23, 1967.

Anderson, Dave. "Clay Prefers Jail to Army." *New York Times,* March 17, 1967.

Applebome, Peter. "Coretta Scott King, 78, Widow of Dr. Martin Luther King, Jr., Dies." *New York Times,* January 31, 2006.

"Belafonte in Paris Assails Policy of U.S. in Vietnam." *New York Times,* March 25, 1966.

Blake, Joseph P. "King Remembered." *Philadelphia Daily News,* January 14, 1983: 46.

Branch, Taylor. "Dr. King's Newest Marcher." *New York Times,* September 4, 2010.

Brown, Hubert G. "An Affable but Angry Rights Leader." *New York Times,* July 28, 1967.

"Capacity Audience Hears Dr. Martin Luther King Lecture at High School." *Grosse Pointe News,* March 31, 1968.

"Carmichael Is Quoted as Saying Negroes Form Guerilla Bands." *New York Times,* July 26, 1967.

"Carmichael Urges a 'Vietnam' in U.S." *New York Times,* July 28, 1967.

Carson, Clayborne, and Tom Hamburger. "The Cambridge Convergence: How a Night in Maryland 30 Years Ago Changed the

Nation's Course of Racial Politics." *Minneapolis Star Tribune,* July 28, 1997.

Chapman, William. "Rally Against the Vietnam War at the Pentagon." *Washington Post,* October 22, 1967.

Davies, Lawrence E. "Dr. King's Response." *New York Times,* April 13, 1967.

Dewan, Shaila. "St. Helena Island Journal: Through Trying Times for Blacks, a Place of Peace." *New York Times,* April 4, 2008.

"Dr. King Accuses Johnson on War." *New York Times,* May 1, 1967: 1.

"Dr. King Defends Action." *New York Times,* January 20, 1968.

"Dr. King, In Prison, Has Virus Infection." *New York Times,* November 1, 1967.

"Dr. King in Stockholm." *New York Times,* April 1, 1966.

"Dr. King Is Denied a Rehearing; Faces 5-Day Term for Contempt." *New York Times,* October 10, 1967.

"Dr. King Is Ordered to Jail in Contempt." *New York Times,* October 19, 1967.

"Dr. King Is Shifted to Safer Jail Cell." *New York Times,* November 2, 1967.

"Dr. King Is Speaker Near Rally by Klan." *New York Times,* December 11, 1967.

"Dr. King Plans to Go to Jail 'Willingly.'" *New York Times,* October 11, 1967.

"Dr. King, Released from Alabama Jail, Plans Soviet Visit." *New York Times,* November 4, 1967.

"Dr. King Starts Peace Crusade." *New York Times,* April 24, 1967.

"Dr. King Surprised." *New York Times,* October 21, 1967.

"Dr. King Tentatively Sets Oct. 30 to Start Jail Term." *New York Times,* October 21, 1967.

"Dr. King to Train 3,000 as Leaders for Capital March." *New York Times,* January 17, 1968.

"Dr. King Urges U.S. to Admit Vietnam War Is 'Mistake.'" *Los Angeles Times,* March 18, 1968.

"Dr. King's Disservice to His Cause." *Life,* April 21, 1967: 4.

"Dr. King's Error." *New York Times,* April 7, 1967.

"Dr. King's Group Maps Civil Disobedience Strategy." *New York Times,* November 27, 1967.

"Dr. King's Tragic Doctrine." *Pittsburgh Courier,* April 15, 1967: 6.

"Dr. King's Wife Says He Is in Good Spirits." *New York Times,* November 3, 1967.

Duberman, Martin. "The Lonesome Road." *Washington Post,* July 9, 1967.

Fiske, Edward B. "Arlington Vigil Held on Vietnam." *New York Times,* February 7, 1968.

Fox, Sylvan. "City's Jews Speak of Renewed Pride." *New York Times,* June 8, 1967.

Frankel, Max. "President Offers U.S. Aid to Cities in Curbing Riots." *New York Times,* March 30, 1968: 1.

Franklin, Ben A. "Dr. King Hints He'd Cancel March if Aid Is Offered." *New York Times,* April 1, 1968.

———. "S.N.C.C. Chief Shot in Cambridge, Md." *New York Times,* July 25, 1967.

Fraser, C. Gerald. "Dr. King Takes 'Poor People's Campaign' to Groups in Harlem and Queens." *New York Times,* March 27, 1968.

———. "Powell Is Heard by 6,000 on Coast." *New York Times,* January 13, 1968.

———. "Powell Says '2d Civil War' Began in Los Angeles." *New York Times,* January 10, 1968.

———. "Powell Won't Run if He Loses Case." *New York Times,* January 15, 1968.

Fremont-Smith, Eliot. "Storm Warnings." *New York Times,* July 12, 1967.

Fripp, William. "King Attacks Vietnam War Cost at Hub Concert to Aid 'Exodus.'" *Boston Globe,* October 28, 1967: 1.

Garrow, David J. "The FBI and Martin Luther King." *The Atlantic,* July 1, 2002.

Gazzar, Brenda. "Civil Rights Activists Recall the Legacy of Rev. Martin Luther King, Jr." *Los Angeles Daily News* via SGVTribune .com, January 19, 2014.

Ghaemi, M.D., Nassir. "The Driving Furies of Martin Luther King, Jr." *Psychology Today,* January/February 2014: 26–27.

Goodman, Walter. "Yessir, Boss, Said the White Radicals: When Black Power Runs the New Left." *New York Times,* September 24, 1967.

Greensberg, Carl. "Dr. King Asks Johnson Defeat, May Back Another Democrat." *Los Angeles Times,* March 17, 1968.

Greenwood, Tom. "Grosse Pointe Recalls King's Emotional Visit in 1968." *Detroit News,* March 14, 1988.

"Guilty Verdict in Mississippi." *New York Times,* October 22, 1967.

Hamilton, Thomas J. "U.S. Policy Scored at Geneva Parley." *New York Times,* May 30, 1967.

Hammer, Richard. "Protest: The Lady Who Came for Lunch." *New York Times,* January 21, 1968.

Hechinger, Fred M. "Ford Fund Pledges Drive Against Racial Prejudice." *New York Times,* February 18, 1968: 1.

Herbers, John. "Dr. King to Fight Bias in the North." *New York Times,* August 6, 1965.

———. "Panel on Civil Disorders Calls for Drastic Action to Avoid 2-Society Nation." *New York Times,* March 1, 1968.

Hill, Gladwin. "California Drive for Kennedy Is Opened by Unruh." *New York Times,* March 17, 1968.

Hofmann, Paul. "Dr. King Is Backed for Peace Ticket." *New York Times,* April 22, 1967.

———. "Foes of Asia War Divide on Mideast." *New York Times,* June 7, 1967.

Huettemman, Jude. "The Night Martin Luther King Came to Grosse Pointe: Pride and Shame Three Weeks Before the End." *Detroit Free Press,* May 5, 1974.

"Hundreds of Negroes View Body of Youth in Memphis." *New York Times,* April 2, 1968.

Hunter, Marjorie. "5,000 Women Rally in Capital Against War." *New York Times,* January 16, 1968.

"Joanie Goes to Jail Again." *Rolling Stone,* November 23, 1967: 7.

Johnson, Thomas. "A Rights Activist." *New York Times,* July 22, 1969.

———. "Cheering Harlem Throngs Walk with Powell in Rain." *New York Times,* March 24, 1968.

Kazan, Alfred. "The Trouble He's Seen." *New York Times Book Review,* May 5, 1968.

"Kennedy's Statement and Excerpts from News Conference." *New York Times,* March 17, 1968.

"King Challenges Court Restraint, Vows to March." *Commercial Appeal,* April 4, 1968.

"King Denies Trying to Merge Rights, Peace." *Los Angeles Times,* April 13, 1967: 28.

"King Hits U.S. War Involvement." *Chicago Tribune,* September 1, 1967: 3.

King, Jr., Dr. Martin Luther. "The American Negro: A Bill of Rights for the Disadvantaged." *New York Times,* November 12, 1967.

Konvitz, Milton R. "Review: Where Do We Go from Here?" *Saturday Review,* July 8, 1967.

Kopkind, Andrew. "Soul Power." *New York Review of Books,* August 24, 1967.

Leiby, Richard. "Declassified documents show NSA listened in on MLK, Muhammad Ali and Art Buchwald." *Washington Post,* September 25, 2013.

Lewis, Carolyn. "Non-Violence Takes Courage: King's Wife." *New York Post,* March 29, 1968.

Lipsyte, Robert. "Clay Refuses Army Oath; Stripped of Boxing Crown." *New York Times,* April 29, 1967: 1.

"Mini-Riot in Memphis..." *New York Times,* March 30, 1968.

Mohr, Charles. "Johnson, Dr. King Confer on Rights." *New York Times,* March 6, 1965.

"N.A.A.C.P. Decries Stand of Dr. King on Vietnam." *New York Times,* April 11, 1967: 1.

Nagourney, Adam. "Rescuing a Vietnam Casualty: Johnson's Legacy." *New York Times,* February 15, 2014.

"Negro Leader Looks Down Road Ahead." *Augusta Chronicle,* June 25, 1967.

"Negro's Lot Decried by Dr. King in Paris." *New York Times,* March 29, 1966.

"New Pol Convention Is a Confused Scene." *Chicago Tribune,* September 2, 1967: 3.

"Nonviolence Tactic Defended by King in Reply to Powell." *New York Times,* March 25, 1968.

"Powell Ends Exile on Bimini to Speak on Coast." *New York Times,* January 9, 1968.

"Powell in Plea for Black Power." *New York Times,* January, 11, 1968.

"Rights Leaders Map Plan for Pressure on Congress." *New York Times,* November 28, 1967.

"Rights Trial: The Klan in the Dock for Three Who Were Slain." *New York Times,* October 15, 1967.

"Riot Report Gets Wide Praise; Brooke Sees Hope for Action." *New York Times,* March 1, 1968.

Robinson, Douglas. "Dr. King Calls for Antiwar Rally in Capital Feb. 5–6." *New York Times,* January 13, 1968.

Rowan, Carl. "Martin Luther King's Tragic Decision." *Reader's Digest,* September 1967: 37.

Rugaber, Walter. "A Negro Is Killed in Memphis March." *New York Times,* March 29, 1968.

———. "Dr. King Gives Up in Alabama to Start 5-Day Jail Sentence." *New York Times,* October 31, 1967: 1.

———. "Dr. King to March in Memphis Again." *New York Times,* March 30, 1968.

————. "Mississippi Jury Convicts 7 of 18 in Rights Killings." *New York Times,* October 21, 1967: 1.

————. "Race Relations: A Hot Spring Begins in Memphis." *New York Times,* March 31, 1968.

"Scene at Pentagon: Beards, Bayonets and Bonfires." *New York Times,* October 22, 1967.

Schmidt, Dana Adams. "Protests Abroad to Back U.S. Rally." *New York Times,* October 21, 1967.

Schudel, Matt. "An Eye on Our Times for 40 Years, Flip Schulke Has Shown Us the Drama of a Changing World, from the Hope and Anger of the Civil Rights Era to the Triumphant Crumbling of the Berlin Wall." *Sun Sentinel,* July 7, 1991.

Sibley, John. "Bunche Disputes Dr. King on Peace." *New York Times,* April 13, 1967: 1.

Seidenspinner, Clarence. "Man's Struggle for Freedom." *Chicago Tribune,* June 25, 1967.

Smith, Bob. "Dr. King Outdated." *Charlotte News,* July 15, 1967.

Spiegel, Irving. "8 Church Leaders Ask Aid to Israel." *New York Times,* May 28, 1967.

Steinberg, David. "Where Do We Go From Here?—Martin Luther King." Book Review, *Commonweal,* November 17, 1967: 215–216.

Tirman, John. "Why Do We Ignore the Civilians Killed in American Wars?" Op. Ed., *Washington Post,* January 6, 2012.

"Transcript of President's New Conference on Foreign and Domestic Matters." *New York Times,* February 3, 1968.

Vecsey, Peter. "From Jim Crow to Obama, Newcombe Has Seen It All." *New York Post,* January 20, 2009.

Waggoner, Walter H. "Shift in Position Is Hinted by King." *New York Times,* March 28, 1968.

"'War on White Man' Urged at Jersey City Negro Rally." *New York Times,* July 19, 1967.

"Washington Negro Leaders Said to Form 'United Front.'" *New York Times,* January 11, 1968.

Weaver, Jr. Warren. "Parley on New Politics Yields to Militant Negroes' Demands." *New York Times,* September 3, 1967: 1.

————. "Politics and Race: Trouble on the 'New Left.'" *New York Times,* September 3, 1967.

————. "Whites and Negroes Split at New Politics Parley." *New York Times,* September 2, 1967.

Webel, Bruce. "James L. Bevel, 72, an Adviser to Dr. King, Is Dead." *New York Times,* December 23, 2008: B10.

Zion, Sidney E. "Rights Leaders Support Criticism of Whites." *New York Times,* March 2, 1968: 1.

## *TheKingCenter.org Digital Archive:*

"A Call for a National Fast by Clergy and Laymen Concerned About Vietnam." Sent to MLK on March 22, 1968.

Belafonte, Harry. "Letter to MLK." February 23, 1968.

Egle, Jack. "Letter to MLK." April 12, 1966.

King, Dr. Martin Luther. "Letter to Adam Clayton Powell." January 2, 1968.

———. "Letter to Jack Egle." April 26, 1966.

———. "Letter to Yves Montand." April 5, 1966.

———. "The Mark of the Hawk." Film Review Printed on Advertisement, 1957.

———. "The Meaning of Hope." Sermon at Dexter Avenue Baptist Church, Montgomery, AL, December 10, 1967.

———. "Message for Morris Abram." September, 1967.

———. Speech in Eutaw, AL. March 20, 1968.

———. Speech in Jackson, MS. Pre–Washington Campaign, March 20, 1968.

———. "Speech to the People of Watts." Los Angeles, CA, August 19, 1965.

———. "Statement Regarding an Attack on the First Amendment." Atlanta, GA, October 30, 1967.

———. "Statement Regarding His Five-Day Jail Sentence in Birmingham." Atlanta, GA, October 30, 1967.

———. "Statement in Geneva, Switzerland, at Pacem in Terris II Convocation." Geneva, Switzerland, May 29, 1967.

———. "Statement" Regarding Kerner Commission and Poor People's Campaign. March 4, 1968.

———. "Statement" Regarding Carl Stokes's Victory. Cleveland, Ohio. [Not Dated].

———. "Statement to the Press" Regarding Riots in Los Angeles. Los Angeles, CA, August 20, 1965.

———. "Telegram to Cesar Chavez." March 5, 1968.

———. "Telegram to Eartha Kitt." January 23, 1968.

———. "Telegram - Invitation to SCLF Celebration." October 24, 1967.

———. "Telegram to President Lyndon Johnson and Press Conference." Ebenezer Baptist Church, Atlanta, GA, July 24, 1967.

———. "Telegram to Robert Sarnoff." February 12, 1968.

————. "Why I Am Opposed to the War in Vietnam." Sermon at Ebenezer Baptist Church. Atlanta, GA, April 30, 1967.

Levison, Stanley. "Letter to MLK." July 12, 1967.

McDonald, Dora. "Letter to Eartha Kitt." January 24, 1968.

Romney, Gov. George. "Telegram to the President." July 24, 1967.

Sargent, Martin. "Letter to Andrew Young." October 27, 1965.

"SCLC Memo on the Ministers Leadership Training Program." February 15, 1968.

Tonight Show Appearance Press Release." February 2, 1968.

Transcript. "Action Committee Meeting." Paschal's Motor Hotel, Atlanta, GA, February 11, 1968.

Transcript, *Face the Nation,* April 16, 1967, CBS News.

Transcript. *Issues and Answers,* June 18, 1967, ABC.

Transcript. "SCLC Retreat, November 1967." Frogmore, SC, November, 1967.

## Web Sources & Online Articles:

Airlie.com

"Anti-War Demonstration in New York City (1967)" Universal News. Internet Archive. Audio/Visual. https://archive.org/details/CEP531.

Banks, Adelle M. "Favorite Songs Carried MLK Through Troubled Times." *Religion News Service* via *Huffington Post,* January 11, 2012. http://www.huffingtonpost.com/2012/01/11/mlk-favorite -songs_n_1200393.html.

Best, Wallace. "The Right Achieved and the Wrong Way Conquered: J. H. Jackson, Martin Luther King, Jr., and the Conflict over Civil Rights." *Religion and American Culture: A Journal of Interpretation,* Vol. 16, No. 2. Summer 2006: 195–226. Jstor.org. http://www .jstor.org/stable/10.1525/rac.2006.16.2.195.

*City of Memphis vs. Martin Luther King, Jr. et al.* Answer to the Defendants. U.S. District Court for the Western District of Tennessee, Western Division, April 4, 1968. http://www.archives.gov/ education/lessons/memphis-v-mlk/.

CNN Library. "1965 Selma to Montgomery March Fast Facts." CNN. com, September 15, 2013. http://www.cnn.com/2013/09/15/us/1965 -selma-to-montgomery-march-fast-facts/.

Coard, Michael. "What Philadelphia Lost When it Lost Dr. Walter P. Lomax, Jr." *Philadelphia Magazine,* October 16, 2013. http://www

.phillymag.com/news/2013/10/16/dr-walter-p-lomax-death-great-philadelphian/.

"Congressman John R. Lewis: Champion of Civil Rights." Biography and Interview. Academy of Achievement, Chicago, IL, June 10, 2004. http://www.achievement.org/autodoc/page/lew0int-1.

"Coretta Scott King: Pioneer of Civil Rights." Biography and Interview. Academy of Achievement, Chicago, IL, June 12, 2004. http://www.achievement.org/autodoc/page/kin1int-1.

"Dr. King's Demands of the City of Chicago (1966)." Center for Human Research and Learning, Loyola University, Chicago. http://www.luc.edu/curl/cfm40/issue1.html.

"Dr. King's Driver Remembers the Reverend's Life, and Death..." *Anderson Cooper 360*, April 4, 2008. CNN.com Blogs. http://ac360.blogs.cnn.com/2008/04/04/dr-kings-driver-remembers-the-reverends-life-and-death/.

"'Dream' Speech Writer Jones Reflects on King Jr." NPR.org, January 17, 2011. http://www.npr.org/2011/01/17/132905796/dream-speech-writer-jones-reflects-on-king-jr.

FBI Stanley Levison File. Part 13 of 14, File Number: 100-392452.

FBI Teletype of MLK Conversation with Stanley Levison, March 28, 1968. http://americanradioworks.publicradio.org/features/king/d2c.html.

FBI Transcript of MLK Conversation with Stanley Levison, March 29, 1968. http://americanradioworks.publicradio.org/features/king/d2c.html.

Gonzales, J. R. "Stink Bombs Cast Pall over Martin Luther King Visit." Bayou City History, *Houston Chronicle*, January 16, 2012. Blog.chron.com.

Harding, Vincent. "Martin Luther King and the Future of America." A *Cross Currents* Special Feature. http://www.aril.org/king.html.

"Harding, Vincent Gordon (1931– )." Martin Luther King, Jr. and the Global Freedom Struggle. http://mlk-kpp01.stanford.edu/index.php/encyclopedia/encyclopedia/enc_harding_vincent_gordon_1931/.

Herschthal, Eric. "King and the Jews—Beyond Heschel." *Jewish Week,* January 11, 2011. http://www.thejewishweek.com/arts/herschthal-arts/king-and-jews-beyond-heschel.

"History—U.S. Marshals and the Pentagon Riot of October 21, 1967." USMarshals.gov. http://www.usmarshals.gov/history/civilian/1967a.htm (accessed Jan. 6, 2014).

James, Frank. "August 5, 1966: Martin Luther King Jr. in Chicago." ChicagoTribune.com, 2014. http://www.chicagotribune.com/news/politics/chi-chicagodays-martinlutherking-story,0,4515753.story.

"Jones, Clarence Benjamin (1931– )." Martin Luther King, Jr. and the Global Freedom Struggle. http://mlk-kpp01.stanford.edu/index.php/encyclopedia/encyclopedia/enc_jones_clarence_benjamin_1931/.

Landmarks Preservation Commission. "The Riverside Church." May 16, 2000: Designation List 313. http://www.neighborhoodpreservationcenter.org/db/bb_files/2000RiversideChurch.pdf.

"Martin Luther King at Santa Rita 1968." Pacifica Radio Archives. Audio Recording. https://archive.org/details/MartinLutherKingAtSantaRita1968.

"Martin Luther King Jr.—Acceptance Speech". Nobelprize.org. Nobel Media AB 2013. http://www.nobelprize.org/nobel_prizes/peace/laureates/1964/king-acceptance_en.html (accessed February 23, 2014).

"Martin Luther King, Jr.: The Last 32 Hours." *Commercial Appeal.* http://media.commercialappeal.com/mlk/timeline.html.

Matthews, David. "Kennedy White House had jitters ahead of 1963 March on Washington." CNN.com, August 28, 2013. http://www.cnn.com/2013/08/28/politics/march-on-washington-kennedy-jitters/.

"Meet the Press: Dr. Martin Luther King, Jr. on the Vietnam War and Racial Progress." Edwin Newman, correspondent. *Meet the Press,* August 13, 1967. NBCUniversal Media. *NBC Learn* (accessed September 5, 2012).

Mezzack, Janet. " 'Without Manners You Are Nothing': Lady Bird Johnson, Eartha Kitt, and The Women Doers' Luncheon of January 18, 1968." *Presidential Studies Quarterly,* Vol. 20, No. 4, Modern First Ladies White House Organization (Fall 1990), pp. 745–756. Published by Wiley. Jstor.org.

Mitchell, John L. "King's Words Resonate at L.A. Church." LATimes.com, April 4, 2008. http://www.latimes.com/news/local/la-me-king4apr04,0,6959402.story.

New York Avenue Presbyterian Church, The. http://www.nyapc.org.

"New York Times Best Seller Listings." Hawes Publications. http://www.hawes.com/pastlist.htm.

Obie, Brooke. "The Spiritual Life: Aretha Franklin Remembers MLK." Ebony.com, August 20, 2013. http://www.ebony.com/wellness-empowerment/the-spiritual-life-aretha-franklin-remembers-mlk-405#axzz2uIKs1i00.

Polk, Jim, and Alicia Stewart. "9 Things About MLK's Speech and the March on Washington." CNN.com, August 28, 2013. http://www.cnn.com/2013/08/28/us/mlk-i-have-a-dream-9-things/index.html.

Pomerance, Rachel. "As MLK Day Approaches, Some Question State of Black-Jewish Ties." Jewish Telegraphic Agency. JewishFedera tions.org, January 11, 2014. http://www.jewishfederations.org/page.aspx?id=74330.

*Report of the Select Committee on Assassinations of the U.S. House of Representatives,* Washington, DC: United States Government Printing Office, 1979. http://www.archives.gov/research/jfk/select-committee-report/part-2e.html.

"Selma to Montgomery March." Martin Luther King, Jr. and the Global Struggle. http://mlk-kpp01.stanford.edu/index.php/encyclopedia/encycloopedia/enc_selma_to_montgomery_march/.

"Statistical Information about Fatal Casualties of the Vietnam War." National Archives. http://www.archives.gov/research/military/vietnam-war/casualty-statistics.html.

Telephone Conversation between MLK and LBJ. November 25, 1963. Audio Recording. http://whitehousetapes.net/clip/lyndon-johnson-martin-luther-king-jr-lbj-and-mlk.

Telephone Conversation between MLK and LBJ. January 15, 1965. Transcript. http://millercenter.org/presidentialrecordings/lbj-wh6501.04-6736.

Telephone Conversation between MLK and LBJ. July 7, 1965. Transcript. http://millercenter.org/presidentialrecordings/lbj-wh6507.02-8311-8312-8313.

Telephone Conversation between MLK and LBJ. August 20, 1965. Transcript. http://whitehousetapes.net/transcript/johnson/wh6508-07-8578.

TheRiversideChurchNY.org

"Thursday, March 14th—Outside Grosse Pointe High School." Memo for "Breakthrough" Members. http://www.gphistorical.org/mlk/.

"Today in Rock: Detroit Declares 'Aretha Franklin Day.'" Rock and Roll Hall of Fame Museum. Rockhall.com, February 16, 2012. http://rockhall.com/blog/post/7321_today-in-rock-detroit-declares-aretha-franklin-day/.

"Vietnam War Deaths and Casualties by Month." The American War Library. http://www.americanwarlibrary.com/vietnam/vwc24.htm.

## Video Sources:

Ali, Muhammad. Interview. YouTube. http://www.youtube.com/watch?v=HeFMyrWlZ68 (accessed February 23, 2014).

"Anti-War Demonstrators Storm Pentagon." Universal Newsreel. YouTube, January 6, 2014.

Baraka, Amiri. Speech at the University of Virginia, January 28, 2011. YouTube (accessed February 8, 2014).

*Brother Outsider: Life of Bayard Rustin.* Dirs. Nancy D. Kates and Bennett Singer. PBS, 2003. Viewed on Netflix.com.

*Citizen King,* a Roja Production for *The American Experience.* PBS, 2004.

Dr. King Speaks at Opera House in Stockholm Sweden, March 31, 1966. *Nordvision/Sverige.* YouTube (accessed January 20, 2014).

*The Merv Griffin Show.* July 6, 1967. YouTube (accessed December 20, 2013).

*MLK: A Call to Conscience,* a T.S. Media Production for *Tavis Smiley Reports.* PBS, 2010.

*Sing Your Song.* Dir. Susanne Rostock, S2BN Belafonte Production, LLC. DVD, 2011.

*STAND.* Dir. Tavis Smiley, Sivat Productions. DVD, 2009.

*The Tonight Show.* February 8, 1968. YouTube (accessed January 19, 2013).

# INDEX

# ABOUT THE AUTHORS

TAVIS SMILEY is the host and managing editor of *Tavis Smiley* on PBS and *The Tavis Smiley Show* from Public Radio International (PRI). He is also the bestselling author of eighteen books. Smiley lives in Los Angeles.

DAVID RITZ, who collaborated with Smiley on *What I Know for Sure,* has worked with everyone from Ray Charles and Marvin Gaye to Aretha Franklin and B. B. King.